PRAISE FOR THE PLAYS OF NEIL LABUTE

REASONS TO BE HAPPY

"Mr. LaBute is more relaxed as a playwright than he's ever been. He is clearly having a good time revisiting old friends . . . you're likely to feel the same way . . . the most winning romantic comedy of the summer, replete with love talk, LaBute-style, which isn't so far from hate talk . . ."

—**Ben Brantley**, *The New York Times*

"These working-class characters are in fine, foul-mouthed voice, thanks to the scribe's astonishing command of the sharp side of the mother tongue. But this time the women stand up for themselves and give as good as they get."

—**Marilyn Stasio**, *Variety*

"LaBute has a keen ear for conversational dialogue in all its profane, funny and inelegant glory." —**Joe Dziemianowicz**, *New York Daily News*

"LaBute . . . nails the bad faith, the grasping at straws, the defensive barbs that mark a tasty brawl." —**Elisabeth Vincentelli**, *New York Post*

". . . intense, funny, and touching . . . In following up with the lives of his earlier characters, LaBute presents another compassionate examination of the ways people struggle to connect and try to find happiness."

—**Jennifer Farrar**, *The Associated Press*

". . . terrifically entertaining." 〕erg

"[A] triumph . . . always electric w on-
strating that even in their direst spo ꞁus.
. . . completely convincing." . . . . . . , *Huffington Post*

REASONS TO BE PRETTY

"Mr. LaBute is writing some of the freshest and most illuminating American dialogue to be heard anywhere these days . . . *Reasons* flows with the compelling naturalness of overheard conversation. . . . It's never easy to say what you mean, or to know what you mean to begin with. With a delicacy that belies its crude vocabulary, *Reasons to be Pretty* celebrates the everyday heroism in the struggle to find out." —**Ben Brantley**, *The New York Times*

"[T]here is no doubt that LaBute knows how to hold an audience. . . . LaBute proves just as interesting writing about human decency as when he is writing about the darker urgings of the human heart." —**Charles Spencer**, *Telegraph*

"[F]unny, daring, thought-provoking . . ." —**Sarah Hemming**, *Financial Times*

IN A DARK DARK HOUSE
"Refreshingly reminds us . . . that [LaBute's] talents go beyond glibly vicious storytelling and extend into thoughtful analyses of a world rotten with original sin." —**Ben Brantley**, *The New York Times*

"LaBute takes us to shadowy places we don't like to talk about, sometimes even to think about . . ." —**Erin McClam**, Newsday

WRECKS
"Superb and subversive . . . A masterly attempt to shed light on the ways in which we manufacture our own darkness. It offers us the kind of illumination that Tom Stoppard has called 'what's left of God's purpose when you take away God.'" —**John Lahr**, *The New Yorker*

"[*Wrecks* is a] tasty morsel of a play . . . The profound empathy that has always informed LaBute's work, even at its most stringent, is expressed more directly and urgently than ever here." —**Elysa Gardner**, *USA Today*

"*Wrecks* is bound to be identified by its shock value. But it must also be cherished for the moment-by-moment pleasure of its masterly portraiture. There is not an extraneous syllable in LaBute's enormously moving love story." —**Linda Winer**, *Newsday*

FAT PIG
"The most emotionally engaging and unsettling of Mr. LaBute's plays since *bash* . . . A serious step forward for a playwright who has always been most comfortable with judgmental distance." —**Ben Brantley**, *The New York Times*

"One of Neil LaBute's subtler efforts . . . Demonstrates a warmth and compassion for its characters missing in many of LaBute's previous works [and] balances black humor and social commentary in a . . . beautifully written, hilarious . . . dissection of how societal pressures affect relationships [that] is astute and up-to-the-minute relevant." —**Frank Scheck**, *New York Post*

THE DISTANCE FROM HERE

"LaBute gets inside the emptiness of American culture, the masquerade, and the evil of neglect. *The Distance From Here*, it seems to me, is a new title to be added to the short list of important contemporary plays."

—**John Lahr**, *The New Yorker*

THE MERCY SEAT

"Though set in the cold, gray light of morning in a downtown loft with inescapable views of the vacuum left by the twin towers, *The Mercy Seat* really occurs in one of those feverish nights of the soul in which men and women lock in vicious sexual combat, as in Strindberg's *Dance of Death* and Edward Albee's *Who's Afraid of Virginia Woolf.*" —**Ben Brantley**, *The New York Times*

"[A] powerful drama . . . LaBute shows a true master's hand in gliding us amid the shoals and reefs of a mined relationship." —**Donald Lyons**, *New York Post*

THE SHAPE OF THINGS

"LaBute . . . continues to probe the fascinating dark side of individualism . . . [His] great gift is to live in and to chronicle that murky area of not-knowing, which mankind spends much of its waking life denying."

—**John Lahr**, *The New Yorker*

"LaBute is the first dramatist since David Mamet and Sam Shepard—since Edward Albee, actually—to mix sympathy and savagery, pathos and power."

—**Donald Lyons**, *New York Post*

"*Shape* . . . is LaBute's thesis on extreme feminine wiles, as well as a disquisition on how far an artist . . . can go in the name of art . . . Like a chiropractor of the soul, LaBute is looking for realignment, listening for a crack." —**John Istel**, *Elle*

BASH

"The three stories in *bash* are correspondingly all, in different ways, about the power instinct, about the animalistic urge for control. In rendering these narratives, Mr. LaBute shows not only a merciless ear for contemporary speech but also a poet's sense of recurring, slyly graduated imagery . . . darkly engrossing."

—**Ben Brantley**, *The New York Times*

NEIL LABUTE is an award-winning playwright, filmmaker, and screen-writer. His plays include: *bash*, *The Shape of Things*, *The Distance From Here*, *The Mercy Seat*, *Fat Pig* (Olivier Award nominated for Best Comedy), *Some Girl(s)*, *Reasons to be Pretty* (Tony Award nominated for Best Play), *In a Forest, Dark and Deep*, a new adaptation of *Miss Julie*, and *Reasons to be Happy*. He is also the author of *Seconds of Pleasure*, a collection of short fiction, and a 2013 recipient of a Literature Award from the American Academy of Arts and Letters.

Neil LaBute's films include *In the Company of Men* (New York Critics' Circle Award for Best First Feature and the Filmmaker Trophy at the Sundance Film Festival), *Your Friends and Neighbors*, *Nurse Betty*, *Possession*, *The Shape of Things*, *Lakeview Terrace*, *Death at a Funeral*, *Some Velvet Morning, Ten x Ten*, and *Dirty Weekend*.

THE MONEY SHOT

A COMEDY BY

NEIL LABUTE

THE OVERLOOK PRESS
NEW YORK, NY

for you, who read it first

"success is the one unpardonable sin against our fellows."
—ambrose bierce

"i love hollywood. everybody's plastic, but i love plastic."
—andy warhol

"rape me. rape me, my friend."
—nirvana

PREFACE

"Go west, young man."

And so I did. Like the 49ers before me (the gold miners, not the football team), I went west to make movies and it was an eye-opening experience. I wasn't actually all that young when I did it—I was an "overnight success" that was ten years in the making—but I made a film (*In the Company of Men*) in relative obscurity, had success with it and then was given the chance to go to Hollywood and do the same thing again, this time with more money and a bigger cast. I loved that experience, which resulted in the film *Your Friends & Neighbors*—thanks in no small part to the brilliant acting and producing of Jason Patric—but after almost twenty years of making films (on both a small and large scale) I have never recaptured the feeling of making that first movie with a cast and crew of friends who did it for no reason other than their love of the cinema. I couldn't pay them very much, so they were all there for the experience and as an experiment in what real independent filmmaking can be.

But spending time in Hollywood and Cannes and various cinematic watering holes in-between did lead me to this place—my first "comedy" as a playwright (or at least the first time I've had the guts to write that word on the title page) and one that uses the world of the movies as its playground. I couldn't have done it without having been at a few opening nights and a few awards ceremonies and having stood on a few studio backlots with a few actors and directors and production executives.

You just can't make this shit up.

Sometimes—most times, actually—life is stranger than fiction and this was one of those rare times that I took a story nugget for a play from something that actually happened out there in the real world.

I was working in London on a new play when an assistant director told me a story about a certain film directed by a certain Frenchman who had asked a certain set of terrific actors if they would have actual sex in his film. They apparently considered the suggestion and brought their loved ones into the discussion. This just seemed like too rich an idea to let slip away; the rest I imagined. I created my own couples and nestled them high in the Hollywood Hills for an evening of drink and dinner and discussion about art and power and sex. Like all good comedic figures, I think these folks are recognizable types—they're not based on anyone in reality and this is not a documentary—so *The Money Shot* doesn't represent my thoughts about making movies or the studio system or anything like that. It simply allows for a lot of jokes to be made about people who are desperate and willing to do almost anything to maintain their way of life. I could've set this story in another city and in another industry, but with my working knowledge of the world of movies, it seemed like the perfect venue for this particular tale of love and lust and greed.

The play had a long gestation period: both my agent and I thought that the best home for this one might be Broadway and so we worked for several years to make that happen. Many readings with various producers led us to chase a variety of famous actors for the show but, in the end, we ended up right where we should be: working with MCC Theater off-Broadway with a terrific director (Terry Kinney) and a cast of remarkable comic actors (Fred Weller, Gia Crovatin, Elizabeth Reaser and Callie Thorne) who were committed to telling the tale and making people laugh. This marks the ninth collaboration between MCC and myself and I feel extremely lucky to have a company who trusts and likes my work enough to have made so much theater with me—it feels great to have a place to call "home" in this business.

The play went through multiple drafts and readings and even a set of staged readings at the Cape Cod Theater Project (in which both Mr. Weller and Ms. Crovatin participated) and so I mistakenly went into the rehearsal process at MCC thinking the script was in great shape. I was wrong (as I so often am in life). It was good. It was fine. It was funny. That said, I have tweaked the hell out of this thing and could keep on doing it forever. Move a word. Lose a monologue. Add a set piece. It never ends with comedy and I and my collaborators have been ruthless in seeking only the best material to put on the stage. "May The Best Idea Win" has been the unofficial credo in the room and that has pretty much been the way it goes. All of us throwing out ideas—even now that the play is up on a stage every night with an audience watching—and I really love the process. I often love the process even more than the product but I'm a weirdo so, please, don't listen very closely to me.

I don't know how many comedies I'll write in my lifetime—it's a tough business and I admire the hell out of those people who seem to do it effortlessly. You sit down to write some kind of "art" but in the end it really feels like some kind of "science." There is a sort of alchemy to being funny; a word more or less here, one additional beat of a double-take there and the audience roars with laughter where we had nothing the night before. Comedy is a mystery and it's been a blast trying to figure it out, but it's also frustrating and demanding and tiring—I'm certainly glad to be sharing my duties with so many gifted people on and behind the stage of the Lucille Lortel Theatre. To hear an audience respond to a line or a look or a pratfall is a powerful kind of elixir I've tasted in only limited doses in my work previous to this but it is strong medicine indeed. I can see why people do it for a living but it's tough and the good ones earn every laugh they get. Audiences are the great equalizers—laughter is a visceral response and you either get it or you don't. After a show, people can be calculated and thoughtful in what they tell you but in the moment and in the dark, they are free to be truthful and caught up in what is happening in front of them—if something is funny, they laugh or they don't. Just like that.

It's pretty damn simple in the end, this comedy thing (if the creation of the universe seems "simple," that is). For better or worse, I needed to do this: write a comedy (or at least try something new). Writers have to push themselves, set the stakes high and keep marching off to new unexplored territories—we're like Lewis & Clark but without the cool buckskin outfits and the fear of Indians at every bend in the river. Mind you, some part of me wishes those great warriors of the First Nation had kicked our asses right back out of this country—after all, look what we've done to it in such a short period of time. Twitter and Twinkies and oil spills were not worth the struggle and bloodshed and loss. I also could've grown up in Europe, probably France, if the "United States" had never come along but hey, that's another story.

As for this play, if you don't get to see *The Money Shot* staged then I hope you enjoy the read. I love reading plays but again—as mentioned earlier—I'm a weirdo. There is nothing like the live theater so at least get some friends together and read the thing out loud. Go to a local college or high school and see a show. Watch one on television or online, even. In person is best but do whatever it takes to experience the pure pleasure of watching words come off a page and spring to life in the hands of a good director and a talented cast of actors. I promise you, you won't be sorry.

In fact, it's as close to Heaven as I may ever get (but for now I'm hedging my bets).

Neil LaBute
September 2014

THE MONEY SHOT

The Money Shot had its American premiere at the Lucille Lortel Theatre (MCC) in New York City in September 2014. It was directed by Terry Kinney.

STEVE   Fred Weller
MISSY   Gia Crovatin
KAREN   Elizabeth Reaser
BEV   Callie Thorne

The text that follows represents the script as it went into previews for the American premiere.

Silence. Darkness.

Blasts of light go off, like a sea of flashbulbs—as if the paparazzi had just stormed the beaches at Normandy.

Frozen in the glare: four people (a MAN *and three* WOMEN*). All dressed nicely, all in their mid 20s to later 40s (the* MAN *might be 50 but is not telling a soul).*

The space itself is a gracious Spanish-style patio that's connected to a lovely home up in the Hollywood Hills. Two big doors (both open) lead into the rest of the house.

The edge of an infinity pool can be seen off in a corner and the whole place is surrounded by lush flora. In case it isn't clear, this is a nice spot. Really nice.

Once the lights have faded they remain in this pose for a second longer, like a Polaroid developing. Suddenly, they all come to life. Mid-laughter. The MAN *speaks:*

STEVE   ". . . suck on *that*, you little bitch!"

They all burst into laughter again—it varies from polite to riotous. STEVE *gets up and pours himself another drink from a nearby counter outfitted with liquor.*

BEV   And then what?

BEV *is* KAREN*'s partner and this is their house*—STEVE *and the* YOUNGER WOMAN *(*"MISSY"*) are guests here.*

STEVE What do you mean?

KAREN She's asking what he said back . . .

BEV I think he understands the question.

STEVE Back to *me*?

KAREN Yes! What'd Christof say to you after you said that? I was still in make-up . . . (*To the others.*) I mean, I *barely* use any, but that's . . . (*To* STEVE.) Anyhow. Steve?

STEVE Oh. Well, he just . . . I mean . . . you know how Christof is!! Little bastard hasn't shut up since he won the *Palme d'Or* . . . so . . .

STEVE *smiles coyly at this and continues tinkering with his drink. A big grin—he's a good-looking dude.*

KAREN Steve! Tell us! Come *on* . . .

Everyone leans forward, waiting to hear the finish to his tale. STEVE *stops and turns. Plays the moment. Sits down.*

STEVE Ok, ok! (*Smiles.*) Not a fuckin' thing.

BEV What?!

STEVE He couldn't! I walked out, right after that. I said that—"Suck on that, you little bitch!"—and then I turned and left, straight back to my trailer. Did not come out, the *entire* afternoon . . .

KAREN I can attest to that!

STEVE Sorry about that, Karen, but hey, you've gotta do something every so often, right? I mean, take a stand or whatever. If not, they see you as weak and that's the start of it right there . . . beginning of the end in *this* business.

KAREN You're not wrong about that.

STEVE Right? I mean, seriously. It's cause and affect. Cause AND affect.

BEV Yeah, for you maybe—actors—but not us. Not everybody else on the food chain . . . *we* walk out and someone's waiting in the carpark to take our spot. *Literally.*

KAREN That's true and it sucks—there's a total disparity between *talent* and the rest of the crew . . . (*To* STEVE.) Anyway, it was no big deal. I actually agree with you.

STEVE . . . for once!

KAREN *Not* true! (*Beat.*) No, I think he gets away with a lot of shit being whatever he is: European, I guess. An "artist."

STEVE Shit! If he's an artist I'm the fucking *Mona Lisa.* (*Beat.*) I don't even know what I mean by that, but you still understand me, don't ya? I mean, that makes sense . . . right? (*Beat.*) *Missy?*

He turns to MISSY*, who hasn't said anything so far this evening. She's just sitting and playing with her hair.*

MISSY Yep. I *totally* get it.

STEVE See? (*To the others.*) Missy gets it. And she really does, too—like, *seventy*-five percent of what I say she gets—and I'm not saying *gets* it as in she understands me, no. I'm saying as in *comprehends* . . . We're "soul mates," Missy and me. (*Beat.*) Anyway, we should get down to it if we're gonna discuss this *sex* thing . . . come to an "understanding" or whatever. Right? They wanna shoot the scene tomorrow . . .

STEVE *is waiting for a response*—KAREN *and* BEV *both nod.*

KAREN Well . . . why don't we . . .

MISSY It's true . . . (*To the others.*) We really are.

KAREN What's that?

MISSY Soul mates. (*To the others.*) I felt that immediately—the first time we made love. Back of Steve's *Porsche*.

KAREN That's great.

BEV . . . *awesome.*

MISSY Thanks!

STEVE It's pretty sweet when you run into that one person, you know? "The one." Doesn't matter at what age, I mean, look at me! Forty . . . whatever. In my forties. I have been through a *lot* of things in my day, *relationships* and all that crap, but I have never felt for any of those ladies what I felt for Missy, first time that I saw her out there on her *boogie-board* . . .

MISSY We met by the ocean.

BEV Yeah . . . I was able to follow that part . . .

MISSY *smiles and nods at* BEV, *who studies this beautiful girl who has somehow landed at her home.* BEV *smiles back.*

STEVE She was incredible . . . running along, up and down that stretch of beach there in Hawaii—you know the spot I mean? Where that one chick, the younger girl . . . she got her arm bitten off by some shark? Right down by . . . what's her name again?

MISSY I dunno. Beth–something . . . was that it? . . . or Becky maybe? *Becky . . .*

KAREN I'm not sure but . . . sharks are very misunderstood, though. I did a voice-over once, for this Greenpeace documentary . . . and they really are majestic creatures. *Majestic.* (*To* STEVE.) Sorry. Go ahead . . .

STEVE Huh. Doesn't matter. I got asked to play her dad in that picture they did about it but no way . . . I'm not ready to pack it in quite yet!! Play supporting bits in some *Lifetime*-looking movie! (*Beat.*) Plus, the money was shit . . . Dennis Quaid took it. He was ok. (*Beat.*) He also played the gay dude in that one picture . . . with Julianne Moore. Remember? You guys *must've* seen that! I passed on that one as well . . .

MISSY Yeah, that was good—and it had that one black guy in it, too. He sells insurance.

BEV Huh. (*To* STEVE.) Why "must" we've seen it?

KAREN . . . Bev, don't . . .

BEV No, I'm just asking. (*To* STEVE.) Why do you assume that "of course" we saw *that* movie . . . because it's got gay characters in it? Is that why?

KAREN Can we just . . . please?

BEV It's only a question.

KAREN *and* BEV *exchange "looks." It won't be the last time this evening.*

STEVE No, I'll tell you why. Not because he's a fag in it—

MISSY (*Whispers.*) Gay.

STEVE "Gay," sorry, "gay"—I figured you saw it because it's a quality film so I just *presumed*. It's my mistake. (*Beat.*) I see all the Oscar nominees on *screeners* that I borrow so I figured . . . what with Karen being a *member* of the Academy . . .

KAREN I was nominated for my performance in *Child of Tomorrow*.

MISSY I loved your clothes in that!

KAREN Thank you! (*To the others.*) Sorry, sorry, sorry.

STEVE We work in the industry.

BEV Uh huh. Uh huh.

STEVE It's our job to support it and know what other people're up to, I think . . . (*To* KAREN.) Anyway, you know I'm not homophobic, right? I mean, that's pretty obvious.

KAREN (*Mock-serious.*) . . . ummmmmm . . .

STEVE Hey, hey, don't even kid! I do that AIDS run, like, every other year, so, come on—and I do the *whole* thing, too, not like just at the start when they're out there taking pictures or, you know— I get the t-shirt and everything! It's true.

MISSY I can vouch for that. I wear one of 'em as a nightgown. (*To* STEVE.) Which year is it again, baby?

STEVE I dunno! '08 maybe. I can't remember. The one with the *rainbow* on it . . .

BEV Ahhh, I think they *all* have rainbows on 'em, Steve—that's kinda the point.

STEVE What is?

KAREN Bev . . .

BEV *just stares at* STEVE—*she decides not to pursue this.*

STEVE *What*? I seriously don't get the reference you're making—is it from a movie? *Wizard of Oz*, or . . . like . . .?

BEV *remains silent—chooses to go over and get a few more olives off a nearby table instead.* KAREN *fills the gap.*

KAREN I did that one year—wait, or was it for breast cancer . . .? (*To* BEV.) Honey, do you remember? (*To the others.*) It was through my *foundation* and sometimes I get things mixed up. I *think* it was some kind of cancer . . .

BEV *glances over at* KAREN, *then turns back to* STEVE.

BEV Anyway. Yes, we saw that movie . . . it was called *Far from Heaven* and it's very good.

STEVE Agreed! Quality. Absolutely. I just don't wanna get type-cast as a homo . . .

MISSY (*Whispers.*) Gay.

STEVE No, I think "homo" is okay. (*Checks with others.*) I'd work with that director in a heartbeat on a regular picture. I *totally* would . . .

KAREN No, I can understand that . . . I mean, look at me, right?

STEVE Sure. (*Beat.*) Wait, what?

KAREN After I came out! I lost a *lot* of work, had all these assumptions made about me and who I am . . . first call I got was not from my family or my agent or some, like, old friend from high school. *No.* It was from a producer on *The "L" Word* . . . seeing if I wanted to do a guest spot!

STEVE Gross.

KAREN We all have to make choices, right? Each of us with our own little *cross* to bear . . . and I'm ok with that. I am. I am A-OK.

KAREN *looks at* BEV *and smiles—*BEV *returns to her seat.*

BEV God! You're always *apologizing* . . . for . . .

KAREN Bev, I don't wanna get into this right now, ok? We have guests. (*To the others.*) Actually, Bev would never tell you this because she's a very . . . well, lemme put it this way . . . she lets her work speak for itself. *But . . .*

BEV . . . Karen, just let it be . . .

KAREN No, I'm proud of you and I wanna say it! Okay? (*To the others.*) She was actually an *assistant* editor on that film. (*Beat.*) Not the surfing one . . . the Julianne Moore.

BEV So yeah, we did see it! (*Smiles.*) A couple *hundred* times!

MISSY Wow! Congrats! (*Beat.*) Is that black guy big? He seems *huge* . . .

STEVE That's cool. Total prestige pic! I really would've done it, too . . . if it hadn't been for the whole, you know . . . gay thing.

BEV *doesn't buy this at all but a look from* KAREN *tells her to "let it go."* *They all sit silently for a moment.*

MISSY Bethany Hamilton!

STEVE What?

MISSY The girl . . .

STEVE Huh?

MISSY . . . from the shark attack. (*To* STEVE.) *What*? I saw the movie, like, *six* times . . .

That was very unexpected— KAREN *and* BEV *study* MISSY *a bit more at this point while* STEVE *beams at her with pride.*

KAREN Good memory.

MISSY Thanks. That's what I do most days, is go to the mall or see films. Plus all the, like, premieres and stuff we go to . . . so yeah. I'm pretty okay at remembering things.

STEVE Nice one, baby! Yes, *her* . . . (*Beat.*) I met Missy right there, in Kauai; I was doing a sequel to one of my franchise pictures. *Soul Crusher*? No . . . *Pain Merchant* I think. *Pain Merchant 3: Hell Hath No Fury*—came out a couple summers ago—it's about this crazy bitch, no offense, who is, like, some sort of *model*-slash-contract killer-slash-high priestess from wherever.

BEV . . . "Hell," it sounds like . . .

KAREN *throws* BEV *another look—only a shrug from* STEVE.

STEVE I think so—I don't know a lot about the bible and stuff—but from somewhere near there, anyway, and my character sends her back to the underworld . . . after this *huge* battle on top of the . . . ummmmm, what's it called? In Seattle? Shit. It's . . . (*Pulls out his iPhone.*) . . . the Space Needle!

BEV Huh. Didn't see it.

STEVE Turned out pretty good—hit a 100 mill' in less than *two* weeks, so . . .

BEV Wow. (*Beat.*) And why were they on top of the Space Needle again? Just curious . . .

STEVE Because it was . . . you'd have to see the whole thing. It's very *character*-driven.

BEV Yeah, but I mean . . . just in your opinion.

STEVE Hell, I dunno! (*Laughs.*) 'Cause it looked cool! We shot entirely on location, though . . . and in the very *first* Starbucks, too.

KAREN Is that the vampire one?

STEVE No! God, that's the *second* one! Huge hit. *Massive.*

KAREN Great. (*Smiles.*) Did you know I passed on that part? The lead vampire? "Ribelda?" They came to me *first* . . .

STEVE Get outta here! I never heard that . . . we got Naomi Watts for it, in the end—we had Kidman for a minute but she jumped off to do something else . . . another *Von Trier* or some shit—and Naomi's great, really sweet . . . I thought she was a bit old but hey. She was very good overall. She kicked some serious ass!! Did a *lot* of her own stunts.

KAREN She's so brave. (*To the others.*) I actually took over her *Revlon* contract . . . did you know that? It's true.

BEV Kidman's actually *older* than Watts.

STEVE *What*? No way!

BEV Yes.

STEVE That's not—(*Pulls out his iPhone again.*) I'm gonna look that up.

MISSY *watches him while digging through her purse. She produces a pack of gum and gobbles down a stick.*

KAREN They offered me five to do it. Five *and* first dollar gross but I *still* said "no." (*Beat.*) I did that *Rwanda* thing instead, which was . . . you know . . . intense . . . plus I was able to start my "*Agua for Africa*" campaign, which is just *so* rewarding!

STEVE   That's crazy! (*Beat.*) I paid for our whole place in Montana on just the *residuals*. Fifteen *thousand* acres up by Yellowstone—we even got some buffalo, don't we, sweetie?

MISSY   Yep. A whole pack of 'em . . . (*To* STEVE.) Is that what they're called? A "pack?"

STEVE   I dunno! They're . . . who *cares*? There must be a dozen of 'em, that's all I know . . . they're *buffaloes*, who gives a shit what they're called? I don't.

BEV   It's a herd, I think.

STEVE   No! That's *cows*. A "herd" of cows.

BEV   Yeah, I know, but I think it's the same for all animals like that. Elephants and cattle. Buffalo, too, I'm pretty sure . . .

STEVE   Huh. (*Beat.*) Do you guys own any?

KAREN *and* BEV *look at each other, then back over at* STEVE *across the coffee table from them.*

BEV   Nope. (*Pointing.*) It's nice up here but it's a little tight for *bison* . . .

MISSY *bursts out laughing. Long and loud. Like this is the funniest thing she's every heard—it just might be.*

MISSY   Ha! Good one!

STEVE   Ok, well, forgive me then if I don't just immediately believe you . . . (*Reads.*) Fuck! You're right . . . Kidman's older by a year or two, *if* this is accurate. These sites get birth dates wrong *all* the time! So . . . (*Beat.*) Karen, do you wanna start this or should I? I mean, we don't have to be all funny about it, we oughta just . . . it's no big deal, really. It's just a *love* scene, right? The two of us doing . . . you know . . .

KAREN That's right! *Technically.* People do this all the time and we shouldn't . . . be . . . out in the *real* world couples make it through these situations and are, you know . . . sometimes they're even the *better* for it!

BEV Yeah. And the rest end in divorce. Or murder.

Silence again. STEVE *returns to his iPhone.* MISSY *speaks.*

MISSY I love it up here in the canyons. It's just so beautiful . . .

KAREN Thanks. (*Points.*) We try to bring special needs kids up for *picnics* twice a month, so . . . it's just our way of giving back.

STEVE Special needs . . . you mean *retards*, right? Huh. Cool. (*Beat.*) What'd it cost? If you don't mind me asking . . . with the grounds.

BEV Oh! Ahhh . . . we paid about . . . actually, we bought it just before the market started to go . . . *schizo* . . . and so . . .

KAREN It was only seven and a half . . . we bought the lots on either side. They were available so we took all of it. (*Points.*) Everything you can see . . .

MISSY It's pretty sweet.

STEVE Yeah, it's cute. (*Looks up.*) I don't love being able to see the freeway down there but . . . I like Coldwater better but this is okay. (*Beat.*) I bought my first place in L.A. up in Coldwater . . . just off of Cherokee. It's really nice up there—now Tyler Perry bought the whole other hillside or something is what I heard so I'm glad I got out when I did, but still . . . it's totally secluded. (*Beat.*) This is good, though. Private.

He nods, then goes back to his phone. The women smile at each other, looking for something else to say.

KAREN Thanks. (*To* MISSY) So, Missy . . . Steve says you're a . . . what? An actress?

MISSY Yeah, I'm trying, but, you know . . . (*Beat.*) By the way, I *love* your website. *So* cool! I think gettting tips on food and clothes from *real* celebrities is *super* helpful . . .

KAREN Thank you! I'm really just trying to keep myself out there. Stay relevant. *Inspire.*

BEV Yeah. And on *occasion* she even still acts . . .

KAREN Oh, stop.

MISSY . . . Speaking of food, we are having dinner tonight, right?

STEVE Aha! (*Holding his iPhone aloft.*) Yes!!

KAREN (*To* STEVE.) What is it?

STEVE See? I knew it! (*Reading.*) ". . . a group of buffalo is called a herd . . ."

BEV What'd I tell you?

STEVE Wait, wait! (*Reading.*) ". . . a herd, gang or obstinacy . . ." I don't know what the hell that last one means but ya see? It's not just "herd." I *knew* it wasn't! "Answers.com!" Best fucking website in the world! (*Beat.*) Guy who sold 'em to us, *that's* the word he'd use all the time . . . up there on the trail. He would call 'em a "gang" of buffalo. Right, Missy? You remember that?

BEV *moves to a counter, picking up her own phone from it.*

MISSY Not really.

STEVE You don't? Honey, *come* on!

MISSY I had my period . . . that first time we went up there and you bought the buffalo. (*To the others.*) I'm very heavy my first day.

STEVE Ugh! What's your *period* got to do with it? Why do you gotta bring that up all the time?!

MISSY I don't always bring it up, I just . . .

STEVE I mean, I'm not trying to be insensitive, but . . . I don't go around talking about my *athlete's foot* to just anybody . . .

KAREN . . . that's alright, maybe we should . . .

BEV *suddenly steps forward, waving her phone at* STEVE.

BEV Wait, hold on! (*Reading.*) "The buffaloes group name is *usually* called a *herd*."

STEVE What?! Bullshit! Which site're you on?

BEV "Answers.com." "Best fucking website in the world!" . . . or so they say.

STEVE Yeah, well, whatever. It says "usually," not all the time. "*Usually.*" My guy—who is a Native American, by the way, and is probably a *little* bit more expert on it than some stupid website— he called 'em a "gang." So can we just leave it there?

BEV Fine. (*Turns off her phone.*) That's fine.

KAREN *nods at this new revelation, then gets to her feet just as* MISSY *points off into the distance.*

MISSY I love being able to see Capitol Records! (*Pointing.*) That's really cool.

STEVE Yeah, lotta history in this town! That's what I love about Hollywood—not like New York or places like that. *London.* I mean, this town is just so fucking *steeped* in history . . .

BEV Uh-huh. It goes back literally *dozens* of years . . .

STEVE Yes! *That's* what I'm saying! (*Beat.*) And I know, I know, those other places have . . . whatever . . . their own culture and a bunch of shit happened there as well, yeah, ok, but not like here! This is the birthplace of *movies*, right?! I mean, that's just so fucking neat . . . to be a part of that!

BEV (*To herself.*) France, actually, but arguable.

STEVE Huh? What's that?

KAREN Bev, please . . .

STEVE No, let her say her thing—are you saying that movies didn't start here? Bev?

BEV I'm not saying anything. (*Beat.*) Look, I'm just someone who *studied* this in school, so . . . don't let that get in the way of . . .

KAREN It's no big deal!

BEV No, I know that. I know that. But there are *facts*, ok, there is such a thing as truth and, and . . . just *truth*. That's all. Cinema did not start in California, whether you feel it was the Lumière Brothers or Edison or his assistant! . . . I mean, there are a *lot* of people trying to take credit for this but the truth is—(*Beat.*) I'm sorry, you're right, it really doesn't matter but when somebody starts going on and on and on . . .

KAREN Steve wasn't going on about anything! He made a comment and that's his *opinion* . . . okay? Not the end of the world! Not some touchstone from which you need to pounce and tell us everything you ever learned about "film" when you were at Brown! Ok?! Yes, it's a good school! *Yes*, you're a very smart and talented person, but not every word spoken to you is an *attack*!! (*Beat.*) That was totally unnecessary and I'm sorry . . . forgive me for that, Bev . . . oops! (*To the others.*) Anyhow, I'm gonna run inside and see how dinner is coming along. I'm trying out a few new recipes on you guys for my site, so that should be—just talk for a few seconds and I'll be right back. If you wanna speak about the *situation* or anything, go ahead . . .

KAREN *doesn't wait for a response—she gets up and moves through the doors and into the interior of the residence.*

BEV *sits stone-faced in her seat.* STEVE *and* MISSY *glance at each other.*
STEVE *shrugs, then turns to* BEV.

STEVE I didn't know all that . . . about movies starting in France.
I just assumed that it was here! I mean, it's called "movie capital
of the world," so naturally . . .

BEV Yeah. I see your mistake.

MISSY I thought the same thing . . .

BEV Somehow that's not entirely comforting.

MISSY What's that mean?

BEV Nothing. Sorry. (*Beat.*) Anybody want some more to drink?

STEVE I'm ok for now.

MISSY I'd take a 7-Up, if you've got one.

STEVE *Diet*, though, right? Because you don't wanna . . .

STEVE *and* MISSY *share a look—finally* MISSY *nods at* BEV.

BEV She doesn't wanna what?

STEVE Nothing. (*Beat.*) She's trying to steer clear of the sugar and
all that other crap they put in soft drinks . . . so . . .

BEV . . . oh . . . okay . . .

STEVE It's no big deal. (*Beat.*) We're watching Missy's weight,
that's all.

BEV Excuse me?

STEVE Her *weight*. We're keeping an eye on it—is that alright, or do
you have something to say on *that* particular subject, too?

BEV No, I'm just . . . no . . .

MISSY I have a tendency to bloat up if I'm not careful. (*Smiles.*) And
I *love* dairy, even if I shouldn't have it.

BEV I see.

MISSY I have a wheat allergy, too, so . . .

BEV God, that's too bad. Sorry!

MISSY It's not a problem—I'm pretty much vegan these days, any-way . . . 'cept for pizza. And bacon. God, do I love *bacon*! (*Beat.*) Otherwise, though . . . yeah. I'm a vegan.

BEV Huh. Well, that's great . . .

STEVE She's twenty-*four* so . . . women have to watch it around that age. Begin to, anyway . . . or else her legs'll get all thick and cheesy in the back. I've seen it happen *lots* of times . . . (*To* MISSY.) Right, baby?

MISSY Absolutely.

BEV That's . . . are you being serious?

STEVE Hell yeah, we're serious! She's a really beautiful woman and to maintain that, to keep that going—especially out there in a town like this one, that values looks and youth and all that shit so highly—you gotta jump on it in your twenties or you're doomed. Seriously. *Doomed.* It's cause and affect, Bev. C & A.

BEV I'm sorry, but that's one of the dumbest things I've ever heard . . .

STEVE Oh, *really*?

BEV Yeah. Pretty much—and I've heard a few *whoppers* in my time, believe me!

MISSY Not to be disrespectful, Bev, but I think Steve knows what he's talking about . . . he honestly does. (*Beat.*) I mean, *look* at his skin!

BEV I'm looking at it.

MISSY Have you ever seen fifty-year-old skin as nice as that?

STEVE (*Jumping to his feet.*) Hey, hey! Jesus, stop, can you?! I'm not *fifty*! Where in hell did you . . . ?!

MISSY Yes, you are . . . *baby* . . .

STEVE No, I'm *not*! Stop it!! (*Beat.*) Where did you hear that, me being that age?! I am currently *48* . . . I don't face the big 5-0 for another *two* years! I mean . . .

MISSY That's not true, honey . . .

STEVE Lookit my driver's license, for fuck's sake! Seriously . . . here! (*Pulling it out.*) *See*?! (*To* MISSY.) I thought we agreed, no talking about *age*! Right?! Didn't we?!

MISSY . . . I know, but . . .

STEVE What?!

MISSY Fine. Whatever. (*To* BEV.) Whatever age he is . . . lookit that skin.

STEVE I'm *48*! Shit! Don't start rumors!!

BEV I thought you looked older than that . . .

STEVE What?! Bullshit!!

BEV I did! I would've guessed at *least* 50.

STEVE That's crazy! I use a 70 sunblock—*inside* the house! (*Beat.*) I look great!

BEV It doesn't matter . . .

STEVE It does to *me*!!

MISSY Sweetie, it's alright . . .

STEVE No, it's important and I want to be very clear about this— I'm in my *forties*. I'm prone to wrinkles—that's *genetics*—and yes, I had my eyes done, I've been very open about that but I'm fighting time on a daily basis and I think I'm doing ok! Pretty damn well, actually . . . (*Beat.*) I mean, God . . . *fifty*?! *Please*.

BEV Ok, fine, whatever. Obviously a lot of Americans agree with you . . .

STEVE Obviously! Including *People* magazine . . .

MISSY Steve was their "Sexiest Man of the Year" six years ago. I was still in *high school* but yeah, it's kinda awesome . . .

STEVE I'm not getting all cocky or whatnot but look at the article sometime if you're . . . doesn't matter. They list my age—pretty clearly—in a sidebar with some other useful stats, and it's right there, clear as day. "42." Which was six years ago, so just do the math . . . (*Beat.*) Might have a copy out in the car, I can check if you really want me to but . . . or you can just Google it.

BEV That's ok. I'll believe you . . .

STEVE Fine, then. Okay. *Good.* Thank you!

KAREN *returns with a tray of shrimp puffs (or something).*

KAREN Here we go! Some treats.

MISSY Oh, yum! Snacks!

KAREN I'm thinking about putting these on the menu at my restaurant in Malibu so I'm *dying* to know what you guys think . . .

MISSY Karen, that is amazing! I didn't know you opened up a restaurant in Malibu! What's it called?

KAREN "The Malibu." (*Beat.*) It's fun . . . I like the play on words.

MISSY (*Not getting it.*) *Huh.*

STEVE Great, I'm starved! We didn't eat since breakfast. Plus, we worked out today . . .

KAREN Yeah, me too. I try to every day. (*Beat.*) At least do Runyon Canyon or something—get the heart pounding.

STEVE Runyon's awesome! We do it, like, *three* times a week—we take the dogs and really chug straight up and down a couple times.

KAREN *holds up the tray, trying to entice the others.*

KAREN . . . anybody else wanna try one? It's bay shrimp wrapped in a filo pastry, and I finish it off with just a touch of my own raspberry coulis . . . (*Beat.*) I took some on *The Today Show* and Matt couldn't stop talking about 'em! He was so sweet.

MISSY *takes all this in, looking doubtfully at the tray.*

MISSY Is there any cream in this?

BEV Did you hear the "shrimp" part . . . ?

KAREN It's very healthy.

MISSY Cool. I'll try a couple, then. (STEVE *clears his throat.*) Or maybe just one.

STEVE Not bad. I'll take another.

BEV Missy's on a diet. Did you know that, Karen?

KAREN Oh, really, that's . . . no, I didn't know that. Interesting. (*Beat.*) I once did a campaign for *Special K* but I don't really believe in diets. Not for my body type.

BEV *and* KAREN *look at each other — the tension is still thick.* MISSY *downs a shrimp puff as* STEVE *sniffs at his.*

MISSY Actually, I just have some food allergies and I'm being really careful about what I eat. That's all.

STEVE *I'm* the food Nazi! (*Laughs.*) Sorry about that . . . nobody here is *German*, right? I don't wanna come off as insensitive or anything . . .

KAREN Ha! Exactly! Isn't that what they call you around the set— "Mr. Sensitivity?"

STEVE Not if they wanna keep their jobs they don't!

STEVE *and* KAREN *have a good chuckle at the idea of this.*

BEV I am, actually.

STEVE What?

BEV German. *Half-German*, on my mother's side.

STEVE . . . what a surprise . . .

BEV What's that?

STEVE Nothing. That's great. (*Beat.*) You look like you'd fit right in on . . . their . . . Olympic team.

BEV I don't follow.

STEVE You know, back when they were all . . . (*He makes a gesture.*) Forget it. It's a *joke.*

BEV I don't get it. (*Beat.*) I actually did do sports in school . . .

STEVE Great for you. Swim team? Field hockey?

BEV No, actually—I went out for football and wrestling. Baseball in the summer.

STEVE You mean softball . . . girls do *softball.*

BEV No. *Baseball.* (*Beat.*) Had to go to court to make it all happen but eventually I was allowed to participate . . . so . . .

STEVE Huh.

MISSY I love baseball. We have a box at Dodger Stadium . . . woo-hoo! "Go Blue!"

STEVE Wow, so you're quite a . . . I mean, going to court so you could play on the . . . you should go ahead and get it over with . . . just have the sex change! It'd be a lot easier!! (*To* MISSY.) Am I wrong?

STEVE *and* MISSY *laugh at this—*BEV *nods and lets it go.*

KAREN Well, I'm very proud of her—Bev's a real *warrior* for women everywhere . . . *and* still keeps herself in great shape. (*Beat.*) Bev actually used to use *my* fitness tapes! I didn't know that until *after* we started dating! Isn't that wild? (*Laughs.*) *Anyway.*

STEVE Neat. (*To* BEV.) I'll give you that, Bev . . . you look pretty fit.

BEV Thanks . . .

KAREN Anyway, we should—what was all the food Nazi talk before? I missed that whole . . .

STEVE Forget it! We were just . . . (*Laughing.*) Missy's watching what she eats and we were having a discussion about it when you were gone, that's all.

KAREN I see. (*To* BEV.) So what's the issue?

BEV No issue, I wasn't saying anything . . . but I don't think you have to qualify it when you make a statement about the Nazis. You don't have to do the whole "German" bit, that's all I was referring to . . .

STEVE Sorry? What?

BEV What you just did—the "Nazi" thing! I'm pretty sure that people are free to make all the Nazi jokes they want these days.

STEVE I don't follow you . . . (*To* KAREN.) What's she talking about now, Karen?

KAREN I'm not sure. (*To* BEV.) Honey, what're you going on about? Just drop it . . .

BEV No, I'm just saying—people say "is anybody here *black*?" or, like, *Jewish*, or whatever to be sensitive to racial and religious stereotypes, that sorta stuff, but there's no need to do it with Nazis, is there? I think we can make as much fun of them as often as we want to—they pretty much brought it down upon them-selves, didn't they? I mean, *I'm* German, and I feel that way . . . so . . .

STEVE I have no idea what you just said . . . (*To the others.*) Am I the only one who can't follow her? (*To* BEV.) What's your deal?

BEV It's not a "deal!" I don't have a deal, I'm just saying . . . God! *Why's* it so impossible to have a *conversation* about anything of worth in L.A.? Why is that?!

KAREN We should be *conversing* about the issue at hand, okay, not about . . . some . . .

STEVE Fine, fine! Agree to disagree, Bev . . . can we do that? (*To himself.*) Jesus.

BEV But I don't think it's *subjective*!

STEVE I really have lost the subject here, so, whatever you wanna say is ok by me . . .

BEV You're just being dismissive now—I have a point of view here! A *valid* point!

STEVE Yeah, I know, you've also got a *crew cut* but I haven't said anything about that yet, either . . .

BEV What the hell does *that* mean?

KAREN . . . can you guys not be so . . .

BEV No, Karen, *no*! I want him to answer that. He comes into our home . . . and he's just . . .

KAREN My home, alright? *Mine.* (*Beat.*) . . . If you wanna get completely technical about it.

BEV . . . you did not just say that . . .

KAREN Yes I did, because you push things! You get onto a topic and you push and bully and, and, and . . . force!

BEV I do not!

KAREN *Yes*, you do, you do it all the time! This is the kind of thing you *live* for—a tiny little mistake in grammar or *syntax* that might hide a cutting remark . . . a *slight* to you and your kind!

BEV Our kind! *Our* kind, ok? You're one, too!

KAREN But not like you!! *You* constantly make a stand for lesbians everywhere and I gotta tell you, it's fucking tiresome . . . really.

STEVE Not to interrupt, but I see where Karen's coming from, Bev . . . (*Beat.*) Sorry.

BEV Fine, if that's how you wanna play it . . .

KAREN *You* do! You make me play it that way! You love this bullshit game of *prove my love* or *we're a couple*—you want me to play it all the time! Every time I'm on Letterman or Craig Ferguson or, or Jimmy Kimmel . . . you're right there, pushing me to make a reference to my "partner" or my sexuality or some fucking thing and I'm sick of it! People do not give a shit and, frankly, they think it's a big turnoff . . . they've got their own crap to worry about!! (*Beat.*) So can we just try and give it a rest, Bev? *Please*?

MISSY I know what you mean . . . when gay people do finally speak up about who they are, it's like all they talk about! I once had a—

KAREN Missy, shhhh, not right now, ok? I need a moment here with my girlfriend . . .

BEV Now I'm your "girlfriend!" A second ago I was your "partner" but now I'm your . . .

KAREN Ohh, just shut up . . . can you do that for me?! Shut your big fucking mouth for *two* seconds and listen to me?!! People know you're queer! Trust me! If we met Stevie Wonder at the *Grammys* . . . *he'd* know!!

BEV Is that right?

KAREN Yes, honey, *that* is correct! He would get it and you know what, it'd be on his back burner before he was shown to his seat . . . I promise you. (*Beat.*) We are lucky enough to live in a town that just doesn't give a shit . . . so long as you are making them money and occasionally I do, and that is *all* that matters. *Period.*

BEV Well . . . that's very cynical.

KAREN It's not me, babe, it's the world . . .

A detente. STEVE *casually watches this contest of wills before adding:*

STEVE I saw Stevie Wonder once, at the Ivy . . . dropped his fork and I watched him look for it for about ten minutes or so, until they brought him a new one. (*Beat.*) Guess he wasn't technically "looking" for it, but you know what I mean . . . (*He acts it out.*) Like this. He came *really* close to finding it, too. A couple times.

BEV I don't know what to say to that, Steve.

STEVE You don't have to say anything, *Bev*—it's just what happened . . . I am reporting the facts as they unfolded. That's all.

MISSY (*Interrupting.*) Karen, the shrimps are really tasty. You're *so* talented.

KAREN Thanks. I think my online readership will like the extra little zip I put in there. I'm just not sure about the restaurant . . . What do you think, Missy? I'm *definitely* gonna put it in my new cookbook, but does it work as a starter? (*Waits.*) . . . anybody?

MISSY I think so! I mean, they're *real* good—meaty but without the fishy taste you can sometimes get. Plus, the pastry thingie . . . what's it called?—that stuff is delicious. It's so flaky! (*To* STEVE.) Just one more?

STEVE Sure.

MISSY Thanks, baby.

STEVE I mean, if you want a fat ass, then fine. Finish off the tray . . .

MISSY Honey, don't. That hurts my feelings.

STEVE Well, I don't mean to, I'm just trying to share my point of view. Okay? Didn't they say that was valid . . . in group on Tuesday?

MISSY Yeah, I guess.

STEVE They totally did!

KAREN Oh, that's . . . (*Beat.*) So you two are going to some kind of counseling, or . . .? Not to be nosy, but I'm just curious.

MISSY Yep. Just the last six months or so . . . and it's really helped our sex life, too!

STEVE You can say *that* again! It's been . . . (*To* MISSY.) You're *so* awesome. (*To the others.*) You know it's our anniversary next month?

BEV Really?

STEVE Yep. *One* year! We made it! (*They kiss.*) I mean, we've *known* each other for almost three, but yeah, married for one . . .

MISSY . . . longest relationship I've ever had and it feels great! Woo-hoo!

KAREN That's so nice. Congratulations! (*Beat.*) I am *dying* to play a therapist one day . . .

BEV Oh . . . so, wait. You've only been together for a *year*—as in

married, I'm saying—and you're already in some kind of a . . .
what? Like, couples . . .

MISSY Uh-huh. It's not court-appointed or like that, though. We just
decided to do it . . .

STEVE I'm into the "big picture," know what I mean? The "five-year
plan," that type of shit—same thing with Missy's diet, as I was
trying to say before. You gotta get on this stuff early or it gets
away from you . . . I'm serious.

MISSY We can give you the number—meets Tuesday and Thursday
nights. Very discreet.

STEVE *TMZ* did a thing on it but other than that it's been really
sweet. (*Beat.*) You want a contact phone, Karen? I'm happy to
help.

KAREN I think that's . . . I appreciate it, but no, we'll probably just . . .
we plan to, ummm . . . (*To* BEV.) Can I tell them about . . . our . . .?

BEV Oh, can we not do this, honestly?

KAREN What?

BEV Discuss our *every* relationship move with total strangers? Can
we at least draw a line in the sand there? Please?!

KAREN . . . Bev . . .

BEV No, I'm serious here!

KAREN I don't even "get" you sometimes! (*To the others.*) One day
we're talking to *Bravo* to do a reality thingie—a *limited* series—
then I turn around and . . . it's this!

STEVE Bev, Karen and I are hardly strangers . . . I mean, we're doing
this film together, plus we both did guest spots on *Friends* back in
the day, so . . . we're not exactly straight-off-the-boat on this one.

BEV Look, no! I'm not gonna be all . . . (*Beat.*) What're we here for
tonight? Really? Is this a *social* occasion or, or . . . just . . . what?!
I thought our little get-together had a purpose to it. I thought you
said this was an *emergency*. (*To* KAREN.) That's what you told me

and so I—I have a pre-dub that I'm supposed to be at but you *begged* me to come to this and it seemed serious so I said "yes." Here I am. Now I'm fine to sit down and discuss all the ramifications of the events at hand but I'm not gonna spew out details from our private life!! I am not, so let's . . . can we please just do this, right now?!

STEVE 'Course we can. Sorry about that, but yeah, let's do it. Get down to all the nitty-gritty. And yes, it *is* important.

BEV Fine. So let's . . . (BEV *'s phone rings.*) Oh God . . . Oh shit . . . the cutting room . . . Michael must've popped in—I've gotta take this. If you'll excuse me . . .

BEV *exits into the house.* KAREN *leans forward to explain:*

KAREN She's kind of on edge lately, so forgive her sharpness—it's a lot of stuff.

STEVE Work, huh? That new Michael Bay film? He can be a real handful, that guy . . . super-talented, though! I *love* his shit!

Suddenly, without warning, KAREN *rushes to the edge of the patio and looks over it. Down toward Los Angeles.*

KAREN OH MY GOD! THAT SOUND! DRIVES ME CRAZY! Can you hear it . . . hear *that*?! (*Holds up her hand, signaling to* MISSY *and* STEVE.) God, look at 'em down there!! All those fucking cars on the 101! I *hate* traffic! That's the one thing about this town—I love my work and the, you know, *fans* and all that, but—the roads are shit!! They really are. You pay *so* much for a home . . . nice home in the hills and people come to a goddamn stand-still, right in front of our gate . . . *right* there! It's insane! Police sirens all the time and those . . . like, *emergency* vehicles . . . and you know what? It's gotten to the point where I just started cheering 'em on! No, I do! If I hear a wreck or people sitting on their horns, I'll come out here and I'll just start screaming, YES! YES! YES!! I mean, if I gotta listen to this all the time, then I want blood and fire . . . know what I'm saying? I don't want a goddamn *Suburu* in the diamond lane with a flat tire! No, fuck that! I want bodies and death and, like, *chaos*!! *That's* what I want!! (*Looking back over at* STEVE *and* MISSY.) It's a nice view, though, otherwise. From up here . . .

KAREN *takes a few deep breaths, smiles, collects herself. She moves back toward the others. She bursts into tears.*

KAREN I'm sorry, that's . . . I don't really mean that! I was just— things between Bev and I have been, you know . . . tense! It doesn't matter . . . (*Beat.*) God, I'm sorry! *Look* at me! I'm not usually . . . this is ridiculous!

MISSY That's ok. Everybody fights.

STEVE Not us. (*Off* MISSY's *look.*) We *don't*! We *disagree* . . . we *argue* . . . that's different.

MISSY . . . yeah, but that's . . .

STEVE Trust me, I have ex-wives! I know what *fighting* is . . . we don't do that! (*Beat.*) Anyway, I totally get it, where you're coming from, Karen . . . it's hard dating *chicks* . . . (*To* MISSY.) No offense, baby.

MISSY No problem. This is a tough business to stay close to someone in. (*A look from* STEVE.) *What*? You know that's true!

STEVE No, you're right—they said that in our group the other night and I agree.

KAREN *wipes her eyes and tries to laugh as she explains:*

KAREN Anyway . . . I appreciate you understanding and just . . .
we're really fine! I promise. (*Beat.*) We've been trying to have a
baby, if you wanna know the—that's a *big* part of this—and it's
been a real killer . . .

MISSY Wow. Congrats! You've *really* kept your figure!

KAREN No, thanks but no, I'm not . . . we're still in the process of . . .

MISSY Oh, sorry!

KAREN That's ok, it's *me*, I didn't even mean to say anything, I was
just trying to give a little . . . context to the . . .

MISSY So it's Bev, then, *she's* the one?

KAREN No, no . . . we're *trying* to have a baby. It hasn't actually
happened yet . . . we're just doing all the—anyway, forgive me!
It's just so hard . . .

MISSY Shit. (*Beat.*) My big mouth!

KAREN Not at all! I shouldn't've said anything. It just spills out
sometimes . . . and I was just venting about the traffic . . . that's
really just . . . I mean, hey . . . that's L.A.!

MISSY No, I'm glad you did! I think it's great! I love children . . .

STEVE Yeah, kids're awesome. Lot of fun. (*Beat.*) Where do you guys
get your sperm . . . is it a family friend or something?

KAREN . . . ummmmm . . .

STEVE Is that *too* personal? I'm sorry, it just makes me sorta curious
. . . how you people do that kind of thing. Without a guy or, you
know . . . a *penis*. Or whatever. *Balls*, I guess . . . technically.

MISSY I agree. It is interesting.

KAREN *thinks for a minute—not sure she wants to do this.*

KAREN There's a whole process that we've . . . it's private, really, the
donorship, but we've gone through a *lot*, lemme just say that. A lot.

MISSY I'll bet! (*Beat.*) We plan to have kids . . . don't we, honey?

STEVE Absolutely! At some point. I mean, I'm in no hurry but yeah . . . if it happens, great. (*Beat.*) Happy to be a dad again . . .

MISSY Steve's got a few already, so . . .

STEVE *Two*! That's all, two . . . God, don't make it sound like I'm running around just . . . I've done the blood tests on those two and all that shit and they're definitely mine but I had to fight a couple cases in court . . .

KAREN Right . . . yeah, I think I've seen a *handful* of stories about that . . . the papers.

STEVE *nods vigorously at this and sits forward to discuss the topic. He's obviously got an opinion on this one.*

STEVE Cover of *Us Weekly* three weeks running!! Yeah, I bet you've seen a few mentions of it out there . . . *Entertainment Tonight* was *camped* on my fucking doorstep for a month at one point! Seriously. Got to a place where *I* was taking bagels and coffee out to them in the morning! Yep. I'd open my door to get the paper— I'm someone who actually enjoys reading the *L.A. Times*, it's got very good sports coverage and the *Calendar* section's been very nice to me, not just Kenny Turan but several of their—

KAREN I love Kenny.

STEVE —anyway, I literally had Mary Hart at the end of the drive- way . . . handing me the early edition, six in the morning! Lady is very sweet—she's got beautiful legs on 'er—but shit . . . come on! That's crazy! Even by, like, movie star standards, that's crazy!! I am not *Cher*, my kid didn't chop his dick off and become a chick or something like that so what is up? Right?! (*Beat.*) This town's insane, honestly . . . you move here and you go bonkers in two, three years, tops. I mean it. It's like a big *asylum* plopped down near the ocean . . . the weather's good, you make a lotta money . . . but we are all fucking nuts and it's everybody, down to the last man. *That's* why nobody realizes it. You don't even know it 'cause you're living right in the *middle* of it! Anyhow, yeah, I got two kids. A boy and a girl. (*Beat.*) I probably don't see 'em enough or spend as many holidays as I'd like to . . . I *want* to, I do . . . something always seems to come up, though. (*Beat.*) But yeah . . . we hope to have a baby . . . Missy and me. Of our own.

MISSY Yep. I couldn't do the Angelina thing and adopt—black babies are cute and all that but I just don't trust 'em. I mean, like when they grow up. (*Beat.*) It might seem racist . . . but that's how I was raised.

STEVE That's not racist! That's from experience and that just makes it a fact. People can say whatever they want but you can't deny a *fact.* It just "is." (*To* KAREN.) Missy's originally from Michigan . . . so . . .

STEVE *kisses* MISSY *on the cheek—* KAREN *waits, then says:*

KAREN I'm not sure I follow—it doesn't matter. (*Beat.*) Cher actually has a *girl* who had a sex change, not the other . . . type . . .

STEVE Really?

KAREN Yeah. "Chastity." I do a lot of outreach with that *whole* community, so . . . yes. I'm a hundred percent certain. He's a guy . . .

STEVE . . . you sure? (*Pulls out his iPhone.*) I can look it up.

KAREN No, I worked with Cher before—she did the title track to one of my films—and I'm quite sure about that. He was originally a girl. (*Beat.*) Goes by "Chaz" now, but . . . anyway . . .

STEVE Huh. Ok, my fault on that one. When I'm wrong I can say so . . . (*Points toward the house.*) Not like *some* people.

KAREN *smiles and nods, then turns to* MISSY *just as she finishes her drink.* KAREN *refills it while asking:*

KAREN   So where're you from, Missy? Detroit?

MISSY   Yeah, originally, but then Idaho. In high school and all that— I was a cheerleader for four years and I acted in some school plays, too.

STEVE   There's a clip of her in one of 'em on YouTube, you should check it out! She's great . . .

KAREN   I will. That sounds . . . what's the play? (*Beat.*) The title?

STEVE   Yeah, what is it again? I always forget the . . . it's by that one guy . . . ummmmm . . .

MISSY   It's *The Crucible*. By Arthur Miller. It's about witches and then some other people, too . . . who aren't witches.

STEVE   *That's* it! Right! "Arthur Miller." He's a pretty good writer, actually.

KAREN   Nice! I love Miller . . . I once did a scene from *After the Fall* for a *benefit* at the Roundabout in New York . . . the "Marilyn" part. (*Beat.*) Sorry . . . you were saying?

MISSY   Yeah. I was one of the possessed girls in the village. I didn't have a lot of lines but the teacher—he was directing it—he turned one of our *freakouts* . . . do you know the play at all? . . . in the courtroom they have us start seeing the devil and going all spastic and, because a couple of us were also cheerleaders and in gymnastics, the director designed this little, ummm, like, *dance* routine for us that grew out of the situation . . . it was pretty cool! He did a light change and everything. That's the part on YouTube . . . apparently Arthur Miller sued our school or something when he heard about it but still . . . it was fun, so—yeah. (*Beat.*) You should check it out!

STEVE   Don't make her look it up, baby . . . do some of it for her!

MISSY . . . no, that's not . . . I'd need my *pilgrim* outfit and everything
. . .

STEVE No! She can imagine that! (*To* KAREN.) You can imagine Missy
dressed up like Winona Ryder, can't you? In the movie, I mean?

KAREN Of course . . . (*To* MISSY.) If you want to do a little of it now,
that's . . . fine . . .

MISSY Ok! (*Gets her phone out.*) Lemme just . . . the music we used
was different. I don't have *Total Eclipse of the Heart* on my iTunes.

STEVE Nah, me either. That's alright, though . . . just put on some
Shakira.

MISSY *puts on some other inappropriate music and drops to her
knees, then collapses. Writhing. What follows this is somewhat
indescribable: part awful, part genius. A dance to end all dances.
She finishes with a handspring into the splits, that's all I know.*

STEVE *claps loudly and* KAREN *joins in—awestruck by what she has
witnessed.* MISSY *pops to her feet and sits down.*

KAREN Wow.

MISSY Anyways, I came here to Hollywood after I graduated.
Steve and I met in Hawaii but I was just on vacation there . . .
I mean, I was with this other guy . . . and then we met and, so,
you know . . . yeah. Long story.

KAREN Huh. (*Beat.*) Well, I'll be sure to take a peek . . . at the clip
I mean. On YouTube.

STEVE She's a really talented kid! Aren't ya, sweetie? (*Hugging her.*)
I got her a small part coming up—you know that new scene in the
drugstore? Where we have the big shoot-out with those two—the
girl who gets shot in the face so hard that it blows her blouse off?
That'll be Missy!

KAREN Umm, no, that's—I had to fly out and do *Good Morning, America*, they were doing a segment on my new fragrance, *Whisper*—so I'm just a little bit behind . . . are these those pages that they just gave us?

STEVE Yep.

KAREN And *what* happens? Sorry, I didn't follow. Missy has a role in our film? Since when?

STEVE She's an innocent bystander. That's what her name is in the script—"an innocent bystander." Guy with that big . . . *shotgun* thingie . . . him? He blasts her and her face goes flying off and her top rips open. We see her—headless there—but she's still standing upright . . . tits out and dripping with blood, because her head is now gone, right? A total splatter-shot. People *love* that shit! And so then she falls over and we go on from there . . . rest of the fight. (*Beat.*) Probably only be a few day's work but it'll have a close-up and everything, and it's nice for her! Keeps building up that IMDb page! (*To* MISSY.) Right, babe?

MISSY Yep. (*Beat.*) They already did a cast of my head. And boobs! That was cool. (*Beat.*) It took 'em a *couple* sessions to do my boobs right but I didn't mind. It's worth it . . .

KAREN Huh.

KAREN *takes this in and nods. She's about to speak when* BEV *returns to the patio. The others wait for her report.*

BEV Sorry, it was him . . . so. What'd I miss?

KAREN . . . ummmm . . .

STEVE We were just talking about stuff. Family things and a little bit about Missy, how she ended up here in California . . .

MISSY We're thinking about having kids, too.

KAREN *recoils at this and gets up to make another drink.*

BEV "Too?" What's that mean?

KAREN Nothing.

BEV Were you discussing . . . our . . . ?

KAREN No! Not at all . . . no. We were just talking about children and it came up.

BEV I see. (*Beat.*) Ok, Karen, whatever.

KAREN It was really no big deal.

BEV Yeah, obviously . . . to you nothing is a big deal. Life is one big gift bag from *Prada* but I'm a little bit more private, okay? I'd like my private life to remain just that. *Private.*

STEVE She really didn't talk about it hardly at all, Bev. Seriously.

BEV Thanks, Steve. I now feel all warm inside and I'm starting to see *unicorns* and, and *fairies*, just hearing you say that!

STEVE Fuck, ok . . . just trying to make peace.

BEV So was it a complete run-down or did you manage to keep even a *shred* of dignity? Name and address of our sperm donor?

KAREN . . . Bev, stop . . .

BEV And it's not David Crosby, in case you're just dying to know! It's *not*!!

KAREN We should drop this and get on with what we're here for, ok? (*Beat.*) Please?

BEV Sure, *now* it's *please*. Now that you've dragged our shit through the . . . shit! I mean, through the . . . whatever! You know what I'm saying!!

KAREN I do, yes, and I'm sorry. Again. *Please* forgive me, sweetheart. (*Edges closer to* BEV.) I really am. Sorry. I had no right to bring up our private . . . stuff . . . with these guys and so I'm asking if you can forgive me. Alright? (*Beat.*) *Beverly*?

BEV Fine. (*To the others.*) Yes, we're trying to have a child. *Yes,* we've agreed that it makes sense for me to carry it, not Karen, even though I'm older, since we don't wanna ruin—as *Maxim* so *deftly* puts it—her "perfect tits" or keep her from any work, God forbid!! (*To* KAREN.) Did I leave anything out?! Should we tell them you've been pushing me to actually *sleep* with someone, a *man*, as we're starting to get more and more desperate since nothing is working?! Can I mention *that* or do we want to keep a few things to ourselves?! (*Beat.*) Hmmm? (*To the others.*) Anything else you wanna know?! Any other *fact* about our extremely *humiliating* stagger toward motherhood? Hmmm? How many times I've spread my legs for this, number of fertilized eggs I can carry? Anything?

MISSY Yeah . . . who's David Crosby?

KAREN *and* BEV *just look at her, unable to even answer.*

STEVE He's a singer. (*Beat.*) Son of Bing Crosby.

MISSY Oh.

BEV . . . no he's not!

STEVE Ummmm, yeah he is. Look it up.

BEV *immediately pulls out her phone and starts to click away on the keyboard.*

KAREN . . . ok, please, let's just get down to the reason we're here tonight. Dinner's gonna be ready in a few minutes and I think we should just jump in here and discuss our little . . . *dilemma* . . . before we get . . . too . . .

STEVE I totally agree.

MISSY I'm ready. I mean, Steve talked to me about it on the way over, so let's do it.

KAREN Great! (*To* BEV.) Honey, can you put your phone away so we can . . .

BEV . . . hold on, I'm just checking on this . . .

KAREN It doesn't matter! BEV!

BEV It does to me. I am telling you he's *not* Bing Crosby's son!

STEVE *Is* too!! Why do you think it was such a big deal when he did all those drugs and fathered a bunch of children with those other lesbian ladies?

BEV I don't know, Steve, *why*? Why don't you tell us?

STEVE Ok, I will. (*Beat.*) Because Bing Crosby is not just a great entertainer and an actor *and* a singer . . . it's not just that. No. It is because Bing Crosby was seen as a real inspiration for a lot of people and as a family man, too! He did those wonderful Christmas specials with his wife and the boys—plus, he did all those orange juice commercials as well!! Americans *loved* him and still do . . . so *that* is what the deal is—it's kind of a massive deal when his eldest son starts fucking every lesbo in sight, no offense—*that's* why it made the front cover of every magazine in America at one point . . . because he comes from good people and good people just do not do that sorta thing!! I'm sorry, but they don't! Okay?! (*Beat.*) End of story.

Silence. The others sit for a moment, taking all this in.

KAREN We should get started on the . . . Christof wants us to come back with a couple of, you know, *scenarios* or whatever that we might . . . be . . . comfortable with. So.

BEV I don't even know where to begin on that one, Steve.

STEVE (*Interrupting.*) Did you find him? On Wikipedia?

BEV Yes . . . he's not at all the child of Bing Crosby. Here. *Look.*

She brings the phone to him. STEVE *squints to read it.*

STEVE People can change that shit—they just go on there and write whatever they want to!

BEV Oh come *on*!

STEVE It's true! (*Beat.*) Mine has a *lot* of facts that are wrong, so . . . my age is off, bunch of my early credits . . . it says I've had *3* DUIs, not 2 . . . a number of things!! So forgive me if I don't just immediately . . .

BEV And Bing Crosby was a notoriously *awful* father, by the way! Just so you know! He was not a good guy . . .

STEVE Oh really?! *Now* you're an authority on "bad dads," too?! "Bad Hollywood dads?!"

BEV Kinda, yeah! I did my thesis film on the subject—a documentary on the fallout of families having a famous parent. So . . .

KAREN She did. That's true.

STEVE So what? That doesn't mean that you're some . . . big . . .

BEV Open a *book*! Come off the beach for two *seconds* and actually read something that was documented by scholarship and, and . . . *research*, for God's sake! (*Beat.*) He was a shitty man to a lot of people, I'm sorry. He made some ok films and he had a great voice . . . that does *not* make him a terrific person. It just doesn't.

STEVE Fine. Agree to disagree, then. (*Beat.*) Are we gonna do this thing or not? Some of us have to be in a make-up chair at 5:30. *A.M.*

STEVE *plops down near* MISSY *as* KAREN *and* BEV *get settled.*

MISSY . . . are we eating soon?

KAREN In a minute, Missy. (*To the others.*) We're here to talk through this love scene—not to discuss the *history* of the world. Right?

BEV Yes, sorry, you're right.

STEVE Fine. (*To the others.*) Okay, so how do we start this? Is someone gonna . . . what?

KAREN I can . . . I mean, I'm the one who got us into this mess. At least, technically! Asked for us to get together and talk. (*Laughs.*) So listen . . . Christof has come back to us—to Steve and myself—with a new approach to the "bed scene," which we're *entertaining* . . . obviously . . .

BEV Obviously . . .

KAREN . . . and so we'd like to discuss it with you guys. Our loved ones. (*Beat.*) So, I think . . .

STEVE Guy's a little prick . . . he really is.

KAREN He's just . . . different. He's European.

STEVE Ummm . . . Belgium isn't necessarily European. Is it?

MISSY I'm not sure.

STEVE I mean, I know it's officially in the European continent or whatever, but I thought that they . . . didn't they break off from everybody else or something? A few countries did. I'm *sure* that I saw something on Fox News about it . . .

BEV No. They're still in Europe.

STEVE You sure? Can you look it up?

BEV I don't need to look it up, Steve . . . I'm alive and living in the world enough to know that one fact: Belgium continues to be part of the continent known as *Europe*.

STEVE Ok, fine! Agree to disagree. God, I thought editors were supposed to be *patient*.

This is too much. BEV *throws up her hands and makes a big show out of her response to this.*

BEV I *am* patient! I have been incredibly nice and patient with you guys tonight—*all* of you—but I wanna get going on this now . . . alright? That's all. Can we, please?

STEVE Yes. Sure. I'm not stopping anybody . . . all I did was ask an innocent question.

BEV Fine. Yes, Belgium is *in* Europe. *Germany*, too . . . just in case you were gonna make another Nazi joke!

STEVE I wasn't. (*To himself.*) Jeez, give 'em a break, they're just *people* . . .

STEVE *turns away a little from the others—he is covertly pulling out his iPhone. He clicks on a few keys.*

KAREN . . . Bev, honey . . . can we . . . ?

BEV I'm done. Go ahead.

MISSY *When* is dinner again? Sorry, I'm getting a little hungry . . .

KAREN It should be very close now, Missy. I'll run in and check in just a minute . . . I'm a spokesperson for Viking stoves so I've got the *best* equipment in my kitchen. *So* precise.

MISSY Cool.

MISSY *checks what* STEVE *is up to and sees an opportunity—she quickly shoves another shrimp snack into her mouth.*

KAREN Yes, so why don't we . . . just . . .?

STEVE Ha! Here we go! I *knew* it! (*Reading.*) "Belgium is part of the *EU*. That's an abbreviation for the "European Union." Not Europe . . . the "*European Union*." Ok? Not the same thing. It's like an off-shoot or something . . . like . . . you know, what the South was trying to do during the Civil War, I think. Like that. But without, you know . . . that whole "slave" situation.

BEV *and* KAREN *look at each other—neither one knows what to say to this. After a stern look from* KAREN, BEV *responds with:*

BEV Huh. I didn't know that.

STEVE I'm just saying . . . people always assume when you're great-looking or, you know, famous or whatever that you just can't possibly have brains, too, but . . . (*Sighs.*) Missy and I deal with this shit every day of our lives and so, yeah, I can get a little touchy about it! Sorry.

KAREN We understand. (*Pointing.*) Thanks for the *tip* about Belgium . . .

STEVE Pleasure! And again, sorry . . . just wanted to prove my point. (*Beat.*) Anyway, Karen, go on.

KAREN Alright, good . . . so. (*Smiles.*) This is just awkward! Ummm-mmm . . . look . . . we're . . .

BEV Karen, we're all aware of the situation so just say it! It's why we're here, or so *I* thought . . . let's quit *dancing* around the issue and just . . . get down to it.

MISSY *sneaks another shrimp puff—*STEVE *just misses this.*

KAREN I *know*! I know, and, God, I've made hard choices a *thousand* times in my career . . . why's it so tough *this* time?

BEV (*To each of them.*) Look, I have a *real* problem with all this, just so you're aware . . . up front.

STEVE And we respect that . . . it's why we're here and not just hiding it from you until the thing's up there on the screen.

KAREN That's right. We're trying to involve our partners in this from the start—as soon as they sprang it on us.

BEV What exactly did they say, anyway? The producers—what's the reasoning here? I mean, I know the movie's called *Jackhammer*. I know you play a beautiful detective who goes head to head with . . . some sorta . . . playboy-slash-millionaire-slash . . . whatever . . . who's . . .

STEVE "Billionaire," actually. That part's been tweaked to reflect the times so, yeah . . . he's a billionaire. (*Beat.*) *My* idea.

BEV *Great.* "Billionaire"-slash-assassin. That much I know. (*To* KAREN) And what happened to *Breaking Point*, anyway? I thought that was a *much* better title . . .

KAREN . . . I dunno. I guess that everyone felt . . .

BEV I mean, it's a thriller, not some . . .

STEVE Actually it's a thriller-*slash*-romance, so . . . you know . . .

BEV Oh, I see. So *Jackhammer* has a double meaning, then, right? It also refers to your dick . . . your "jackhammer." Correct? Is that a sexual reference that you've cleverly tucked into the title, Steve?

STEVE *thinks about this—glances at* MISSY—*then responds:*

STEVE I mean, no . . . not specifically. It's a bit more *subtle* than that . . . it's like a double intenuendo. I think it's fun. (*Beat.*) And I don't mean to be . . . but he's not really an "assassin," per se. Not technically.

BEV No?

STEVE No . . . he's more of a "mercenary," really. That's the word I'd use to describe "Jack." "Mercenary."

BEV I'm sorry. Wait . . . his name's "Jack" now? Really?! They *actually* changed your character's name to "Jack?"

STEVE Duh! I mean—where do you think the title comes from?! He's not some guy who works *construction*! (*Laughs.*) Right, Missy?

STEVE *looks over at* MISSY, *who has just popped another of those shrimp things into her mouth. She grins at him.*

MISSY Mmmmm-hmmmm.

STEVE Dude's name is "Jack Hammer," thus *JACK-HAMMER.* I think it's great and it looks bitchin' on the posters that they mocked up so far. (*To* KAREN.) Did you see those yet, Karen?

KAREN Yeah. Looking good. Except for . . . the . . .

STEVE What?

KAREN Nothing, no, I just . . . it's a small thing that I'm . . . (*Beat.*) We should try to keep on track here. They're expecting a call.

STEVE No, please—I'm also an "exec producer" on this, as you know . . .

KAREN . . . Oh, I do know that . . .

STEVE So yeah, I can step outside the role at any time and see the bigger picture so, please, use me as a *resource.* Go ahead.

KAREN It's just—my agent should really be the one to say something, but—I just hate it when, you know, they have the two photos of us—like the ones they've used, with you on one side, me on the other—but up there on the top, they have our names reversed.

STEVE I got it right here. (*Brings out his iPhone again.*) And?

KAREN My name over your head and then yours over mine. I just think that's so weird! And confusing. I also don't love our names in red . . . but other than that . . .

STEVE . . . yeah . . . it's a *billing* issue . . .

BEV . . . are we *really* talking about this? How you guys look on the *poster?*

KAREN Oh, I'm sorry . . . is this not interesting enough for you?!

BEV Ahh, nothing to do with interesting but more to do with how fucking petty and, and . . . *narcissistic* it is! That's all.

KAREN I see.

BEV I mean, to us "common" folk.

KAREN Oh shit! I used that word one time, *once*, and you fucking pounced on it . . . like . . .

BEV You have *no* respect for anyone on the crew! *None*!!

KAREN That's so not true!

BEV It's completely true!

KAREN Bullshit! I brought *brownies* in on the first day for the make-up girls . . .

STEVE Those were good! (*To* KAREN.) . . . you made those?

BEV So what?! You are so—you actually let them refer to you as "talent" when they talk about you! As "*the* talent!!"

KAREN It's an industry term!

STEVE . . . it really is, Bev . . . I use it, too . . .

BEV *Who* cares? It's the most pretentious shit I've ever heard . . . "talent!" My God, like you don't get enough free crap laid at your feet, every day, every fucking day! The trailers and, and agency gifts and photos in magazines . . . but it's never enough, is it? Not when you've got *talent*! When you are *talented*!! It's never *ever* enough!!

KAREN . . . I don't even *know* you right now . . .

A long moment of tense silence as MISSY *sneaks another few appetizers into her handbag and gets to her feet.*

MISSY I'm just gonna pop inside and powder my nose . . . (*Grabs up her purse.*) Is that ok?

STEVE Fine.

MISSY *exits as* BEV *and* KAREN *begin to square off a bit.*

KAREN . . . I think you check your own credits on every movie pretty closely, ok? You went ballistic on that one . . . gay cheerleading indie you did. Remember that? Huh? (*Beat.*) You made them change the *print* before it could be screened at Sundance!

BEV Yeah, but that wasn't about the poster . . . not about how big my *face* was on the . . .

KAREN *Who* cares?! It's part of the business!

BEV This was about me *receiving* credit! My actual *credit*! Not about the point size or the font type or, or . . . no! I was fighting for *A* credit!

KAREN And what do you think we're talking about here, huh?! Getting credit! I don't wanna have Steve's *name* over my *head*!!

STEVE It's a billing issue . . .

KAREN . . . same thing I fought for when they had Beyonce's name over my head and vice versa in that *TRESemmé* ad . . . and I didn't hear you complaining then!! Not when you got to come to the photo shoot! I had to *pull* you off her!!

BEV They had me down as one of the *designers*! It was a *mistake*, ok?! An actual mistake! Not just some . . . *subjective* . . . bullshit . . .

KAREN Oh, so my *name* is bullshit? Me getting a credit that I deserve, that I have *fought* for in an industry that despises strong women . . . or *any* women, for that matter!! You think *that's* bullshit, Bev?!

STEVE I don't think this is helping anything . . . (*Beat.*) Ladies, can we just . . .?

BEV Your name is *six* inches high . . . at the top of the poster! Who gives a shit on which *side* of the poster it's on?! I mean . . .

KAREN *I* DO! *I* GIVE A SHIT, AND SO SHOULD YOU!! I am not at all ashamed that I am trying desperately to hold onto a career here!!

BEV Yeah, because you're selfish! That's all this is . . . you being selfish!

KAREN You're right . . . so selfish that I put down almost *two* million in cash on this place, a place for *us*, Bev! For me and my *lover*! 'Cause I'm so fucking *selfish*!!

BEV I put down everything I had, too! All my savings, so don't try to make me feel . . .

KAREN Yes, I know, and I've never said anything about that . . .

BEV Oh, is there something to *say* about it? I didn't realize that!

KAREN No, I just want you to shut up and be a little more grateful
sometimes . . . that's all. Grateful.

BEV "Grateful?!"

KAREN Yes, and I chose that word very *very* carefully.

BEV I should be "grateful" now?! What, that I get to live in your
beautiful house, with you, the wonderful, youthful movie star—

KAREN . . . you're getting warmer . . .

BEV *has had enough of these exchanges with* KAREN. *Puts a finger in*
KAREN*'s face to make her point this time.*

BEV I can be outta here in an *afternoon* if that's what you want.

KAREN Do not tempt me.

BEV I'll seriously go pack my stuff right now and be gone if
that's what you want—I am *not* gonna be a *burden* on anybody!
God!!

KAREN . . . I didn't say that . . .

BEV Especially someone who lives in *fear* all the time . . .

KAREN Stop this . . .

BEV You're a *poster girl* for this town!

KAREN Stop it!!

BEV All smiles but afraid of your own fucking shadow!

KAREN Stop!!

STEVE . . . actually . . . we can probably just do this over the phone . . .

BEV Hey, hey, you opened the door here, so . . . let's . . .

KAREN Bev! Stop!!

BEV No! NO!! You wanted to do this so let's just get it all out . . .

KAREN JUST SHUT UP! SHUT UP!! SHUT-THE-FUCK-UP!!!

And BEV *does, just like that.* KAREN *goes and puts both arms around* BEV *and hugs her tight. One little burst of emotion from both of them, followed by a lingering kiss.*

MISSY *returns, chewing and wiping her lips with a napkin. She tosses it into the bushes as she walks to her seat—she glances at* STEVE, *trying to figure out what happened while she was gone.*

KAREN Bev's right, you know—about being afraid. *I* am, all the time. (*Beat.*) This town makes you feel that way, constantly . . . the *second* you make it or whatever, you're sure it's gonna go away or, or . . . not be enough or makes you want more. You worry how you'll ever be able to keep what you've got . . . or worse, that people will finally realize that you're a fraud. We're out there on the red carpet, smiles on our lips, and we are fucking terrified! (*Beat.*) There's always someone better and younger and hotter. Flavor of the *minute.* And the moment they ask you to play a "mom" you know it's over . . . and so you struggle to be unique or necessary or a star in *Korea,* even . . . anything! Then a couple films don't open well or you're canceled midseason and boom! There you are, dressed in *sequins* and out on the dance floor—begging America to please not eliminate you this week!

STEVE Jesus.

KAREN 'S kinda pathetic . . . (*Beat.*) Anyway, sorry! Shit, we're *really* putting on a show here tonight! Aren't we?

BEV This is what happens when you've got *two* Margo Channings living under one roof!

STEVE . . . I don't know who that is—I'm assuming it's some sorta gay *icon,* but whatever.

BEV *What*? Seriously?

KAREN It's from *All About Eve*. The Bette Davis character is named that. Margo Channing. (*Imitating her.*) "Fasten your seatbelts, it's going to be a bumpy night!"

The two women kiss and snuggle again. STEVE *and* MISSY *watch them, glancing at each other uncomfortably.*

BEV . . . love you.

KAREN You too.

MISSY Wow, that's weird. You kiss just like a guy would. (*To* KAREN.) Bev does, I mean.

KAREN Really? I never noticed . . .

BEV What does that even mean?

MISSY No, it's obviously a *compliment* . . .

BEV It is?

MISSY Sure! I'm straight so I tend to like the ways guys do things . . . I'm just saying . . . when you put your arms around her, you look like a man. Especially from behind, with the . . . you know. The way you take charge.

BEV Huh. Well, "thanks," I guess.

BEV *makes eye contact with* MISSY—*it lingers for a bit longer than* STEVE *is happy with so he jumps in:*

STEVE I see what you mean, baby. (*Beat.*) Missy's really got an eye for detail and so do I. *Lots* of directors tell me that . . .

BEV Then maybe you should direct.

STEVE Yeah, I might one day. Maybe a commercial or something, just to try it out—they've got special Oscars for short movies, too; I could see myself winning one of those.

The others look at KAREN. *Smile.* BEV *turns back to* STEVE.

BEV Well, you know where to get an editor!

STEVE True! (*Beat.*) But you just do assisting, right? Isn't that what you said?

BEV I do *both*—depends on the size of the project, usually, but I do both.

KAREN She's really great.

STEVE I'll check out the cheerleading thingie—what's it called again?

BEV *Little Angels.*

STEVE Cool. Sounds sexy.

KAREN It is . . .

BEV But in a very beautiful way. It's this coming-of-age story . . . about a young . . . headstrong girl who's about to . . .

STEVE Yeah, but there is sex in it, correct? I mean, like, *between* the cheerleaders? (*To* KAREN.) I'm just guessing from the way you described it . . .

BEV . . . ummm, yes, there is one . . . *brief* . . .

STEVE Okay, sweet. I'll Netflix it.

STEVE *pulls out his iPhone and pushes a couple buttons.*

Karen, go ahead, let's keep this thing moving—we gotta let them know soon. We have a major scene to do in the morning. There, it's now in my *queue*. (*Reading.*) Oh, nice. Three stars! Anyway. Karen?

KAREN Right! So . . . about this love scene . . .

BEV I looked at those pages in the script one more time, before you guys got here, and I gotta say there's not that much there— I mean, as described by the *six* writers. It says: "*They melt into bed and become one.*"

STEVE . . . yeah . . . and . . .?

BEV So, what's the big deal? I mean, why're they suddenly turning this into some . . . *massive* . . . sex scene? I don't understand.

KAREN . . . it's *been* brewing for a while now . . .

STEVE Listen, not to be crass, but Karen and I could both use a hit right about now!! *I* feel like I'm *constantly* fighting my, you know, my image and yes, I've done a little bit of rehab, been arrested a few times . . . Jesus!! *You* try living with the pressure, ok?!! You try it!! (*Beat.*) And Karen, too! It's not just me! Your last big one since you came out was that Tom Hanks thing . . .

KAREN I love Tom.

STEVE . . . and that's, like, however many years ago. I mean, really. (*To* BEV *and* MISSY.) We *need* this . . . this is huge for us, and I actually think it's good for the whole . . . you know . . . film. (*Beat.*) This is new, it's fresh, it's edgy . . . and it really works for my character!

BEV Yeah? Why's that?

STEVE It's hard to keep thinking up reasons for me to take my shirt off—getting naked's a totally *organic* way for that to happen!

BEV I see.

STEVE I have to keep an eye on the whole thing, the bigger picture— did I tell you that I'm an "exec producer" on this flick?

BEV Yeah, I think you mentioned it. (*Beat.*) Now, what Karen has told me . . . at least *led* me to believe . . . they're asking for the two of you to actually have sex. On camera.

KAREN . . . I mean . . . they're . . . *exploring* the . . .

STEVE . . . yeah, that's it. More or less.

BEV How much "more" or "less?"

A look between KAREN *and* STEVE. *Finally* STEVE *blurts out:*

STEVE Listen . . . it's the Belgian! That little asshole's the guy who thought this up!

KAREN I'll second that—he's the one who came to my trailer and proposed it. I mean, it makes a certain amount of sense, he's the director . . . but that's where the whole . . .

STEVE Plus he gets a writing credit! *Fucker*.

KAREN Anyhow . . . yes. The money people like it, feels it pushes the envelope in a new way that's inevitable and, and . . . since Steve and I are pretty much household names . . . we'll get a lot of internet buzz and coverage in the legit press as well. So. (*Beat.*) It's never been done by Americans before, in a movie backed by the majors.

BEV Yeah, but, I mean . . . that's an instant NC-17! I've faced this before and the sex wasn't even real . . . !!

STEVE That's all covered! We just *suggest* it in the domestic prints . . . the hard stuff will only appear in Europe and, like, select Asian markets. It then comes out a few months later on the "director's cut" of the DVD stateside and we rake it in on *that* end, too . . .

KAREN It made sense to me when he described it. I mean, the curiosity factor alone is . . . and I'm seriously looking into the idea of a line of sex toys. High-end. Dainty. From recycled materials. I've never seen an actor endorse those yet . . . could be a *massive* deal, Bev . . . I mean, the sort of deal we could *retire* on.

STEVE The whole thing's a pretty gutsy move, I think. Across the board.

BEV I'm sure you do. Plus, it's for your art.

STEVE I mean, yeah . . . for our *film*. And not just that but a place in cinema history. (*Beat.*) Major stars have *never* had sex on screen before, not the real kind, anyway! (*Laughs.*) So far as anybody knows . . .

BEV Well, maybe there's a reason for that . . . Maybe it's not supposed to happen! It's not supposed to be *real*—you're not an *assassin* in real life, are you, Steve?

STEVE . . . no . . .

BEV So why the hell do you have to have *real* sex, then? Answer me that . . . I mean . . . how is this not just *porn*?

STEVE Jesus, no, porn is different!!

BEV *How*?

STEVE Porn is, like, dirty, and, and just . . . it's "porn!"

BEV It's *sex* on *camera* and that's what *this* is! This is worse, actually, because you are trying to make it something it's not, trying to tell yourself it's "important" and bullshit like that when you really just wanna get off with each other and have people watch . . . no, more than that, not just watch . . . you want them to pay for it. *Pay* for the *privilege* of watching you two—not just some no-name actors but two "stars"—to prove to yourselves and your agents and the paying public that you've still got it, that you still *mean* something . . . it is self-adoring shit, that's all this is! It's public masturbation!!

STEVE Wrong! No . . . NO!! It's classy!!! (*To* KAREN.) Can you help me out here, please? *Karen*?

KAREN What am I supposed to say?

STEVE She's your problem, not mine—I already got Missy to agree to it before we came here.

BEV Wow . . . now I'm a "problem." It just keeps getting better!

KAREN . . . he didn't mean that . . .

STEVE Yeah, well, *I'm* not the one who keeps jamming my finger in the dike on this one. As it were . . .

BEV You know what? One more crack outta you and I'm gonna walk, ok? Back inside the house and I'm done. You hear me?

STEVE *throws his hands up in the air in mock surrender.*

STEVE   Yep. Got it. (*To the others.*) You two are my witnesses here . . . all I said was . . .

MISSY   . . . maybe we should just make a list.

BEV   A "list?"

Everybody turns and looks at MISSY. *She smiles at them.*

MISSY   Of things they can and can't do. If you feel that something is totally wrong or off-limits then we'll write it out in black & white so there's no question about it later. "*No* sixty-nines?" Fine. Double-ended dildos? OK! Either way, just jot it down and then we know . . . (*To the others.*) Or whatever.

A general nod of approval from everybody. Even from BEV.

KAREN   Finally! A good idea!

STEVE   Yeah, let's just do a list!

BEV   Ummm . . .

KAREN *sits up in her seat and begins—*STEVE *jumps back on his iPhone to get some info.*

KAREN   Alright, so . . . if we just throw out a few, I dunno, *positions* or, like . . . specific . . . things . . . can we just rate them as a group as to whether they're ok or not. Do we agree? (*Waits.*) Fine. So let's jump right in and . . . does anyone . . .?

MISSY   No anal.

KAREN   (*Flustered.*) Oh! Whoa! . . . ummmm . . . ok . . . I was gonna start with an easy one, but hey . . . *anal* is good, too . . .

MISSY I mean, unless you really want to, then it's fine. It's just a
health thing for me.

KAREN Perfect. So lemme . . . (*She gets up.*) I'll write that down . . .

MISSY Oh, and just to be clear? I mean, like, no tongue in your ass
and then in your pussy . . . that's what I meant. Steve can fuck you
in the ass—if you guys want—and obviously he'll use a condom
and all that, so that's fine . . . I just think to be going back and
forth down there too many times, and with his tongue . . . that's
a great way to get sick or catch something. (*Beat.*) *Trust* me.

KAREN *returns to her seat with a pad of paper and a pen.*

STEVE Missy's totally health conscious! I mean, God, *lookit* that
body! Right?

KAREN That's great . . . (*Beat.*) So, "no anal . . . "

STEVE Anyhow . . . I agree! No need for that kinda stuff so how 'bout
we put that on top of the "no" list? "No tongue in ass followed by
tongue in vagina." Or vice versa. Good. What else? (*Beat.*) Oh, put
me down for no animals or that type of thing . . . like, *gerbils* and
shit. *What*? He's European-yoon-yonian, so . . . you never know.

BEV I don't think I can do this . . .

KAREN Bev, honey, please . . .

BEV No, I don't wanna be a part of this!

KAREN Come on . . . let's just go through all the stuff we can think
of quickly and we'll be done then, and not another *word* about it.
I promise. (*Beat.*) PROMISE.

BEV God, whatever! Fine, two minutes. Go!

KAREN Thank you. (*To the others.*) Ok . . . blowjob?

STEVE I'm fine with those.

MISSY Yep. That's cool.

BEV That's . . . is he going to . . . you know? Cum?

STEVE Depends on how good she is!

He turns and high-fives with MISSY. BEV *is not amused.*

BEV Hey, I'm *serious*.

STEVE Sorry, but, it's kinda true, though . . . It's C & A, Bev, C & A.

BEV Fine, let's say she's good at it. She was with men before I met her so I'm assuming she can . . . do that . . .

KAREN I can. (*To the others.*) Don't know if I'd get an "A" or not in *Entertainment Weekly* but I can hold my own . . .

BEV *Great!* Ok, so now we know that. Karen can give blowjobs . . . (*Beat.*) And if she makes Steve . . . *ejaculate* . . . then what?

KAREN I dunno. (*To the others.*) Thoughts?

STEVE I guess . . . we just . . . ummmmm . . .

MISSY Do you swallow?

KAREN I'm sorry?

MISSY Swallow? In the old days—back when you were a hetero— did you swallow or spit? I mean, like, on average . . .

KAREN I consider myself "bi," but whatever . . .

MISSY And I consider myself an "actress," but hey, we all gotta be realistic here . . . (*Beat.*) Sorry, I just think that term's kinda bogus, that's all.

KAREN What does that mean?

MISSY It means "if the shoe fits . . ." or however that saying goes . . . (*To* STEVE.) Honey?

STEVE I dunno. You want me to look it up?

MISSY No, you know that one! "If the shoe fits, wear it." That's how it goes, right?

STEVE Yeah. I'm pretty sure that's it . . .

MISSY Anyways. (*To* KAREN.) "Bi" just means you don't wanna have to choose. That's fine, but just say it. Don't try and give the thing some fancy name . . . it's like "sex addiction." I mean, come on! You wanna have *lots* of sex, that's what *that* means! Who doesn't? So join the club but, like, stop making up excuses to hide behind . . . or whatever. That's what I think.

KAREN Umm . . . ok. (*To the others.*) Both, I guess. I've tried both. (*To* BEV.) *Before* we met.

MISSY Cool. I swallow but that's a choice.

STEVE You should see the way this kid . . . Jesus, it's amazing! She can actually—

KAREN Steve, no! (*Beat.*) Just . . . *no.*

STEVE Ok. Your loss.

KAREN Fine. (*Beat.*) So will I swallow his cum if it comes to that, that's the question . . . ?

MISSY Yeah, or, you know . . . let him splash it on you somewhere? Your face or tits—or in your hair, even?

KAREN Oh, God.

MISSY It's called the *money shot.*

STEVE Ha! She means in X-rated pictures—they use it in other films too now, for the big action scenes or the close-up—but it still sorta applies here, though, right? I mean . . .

MISSY I'm fine with that if it's okay by you . . .

KAREN I hadn't actually . . . *lemme* think about that . . . Bev, you wanna jump in here?

BEV I don't care. Do whatever. Take a *shower* in the stuff if that's what you want . . .

KAREN That is not helpful!

BEV . . . well . . .

KAREN We're trying to be grown-up about this!

BEV Really? Us sitting around before dinner deciding what our partners can or can't do to each other sexually . . . that we're willing to let slide for a *movie*—that's "grown-up?" Is it?!

KAREN Fuck . . . you're *such* a spoilsport . . .

BEV No, actually, I'm trying my damndest to protect a relationship that I care very deeply about . . . that my "partner" or my "girl-friend" or my . . . whatever the fuck you decide to call us next . . . does not appear to give two shits about! *That's* what I'm trying to do!!

KAREN You know, maybe it's better if you have *no* idea what we do . . . I thought we could do this but I'm starting to think that maybe Steve and I should just . . . go for it and do what we feel like on the day. That might be best . . . (*To the others.*) Why don't I go and see if dinner's . . .?

BEV NO! NO WAY!! (*Beat.*) We are gonna finish this right now, no matter how painful it is . . . today. This evening. *Now.* (*To* KAREN.) Come on, keep going! You wanna *bang* this guy so fucking badly, then let's hear about it!

KAREN Bev, don't be a . . . stop with the *drama*! NO MORE DRAMA! I get enough drama on set . . .

STEVE . . . you're not talking about me, are you? Because I just fight for what's best for the film . . . I'm an exec producer . . .

KAREN EVERYBODY STOP NOW! REALLY, JUST STOP IT!! (*Beat.*) I don't want any comments . . . just a "yes" or "no." That's *all*. Okay? (*Waits a beat.*) Great. So, lemme get this straight . . . is actual sex ok? And I mean penetration, that sort of "sex?" Is it?

STEVE I'm fine with it.

MISSY Me too. You mean "Doggy" or, like, you guys on a chair or what . . .?

KAREN No questions! "Yes" or "no?"

MISSY Then "yes." I was just curious.

KAREN Bev?

BEV Whatever you decide.

KAREN I said "yes" or "no?!" "*Yes*" or "*no*?!!"

BEV Then "no." I don't want you doing that.

KAREN God . . . you're not even gonna wrestle with it . . . just "no." Ok. You have the right to veto and so you did, and it's "no," right? Just a big *fat* "no."

BEV Yes. I mean, that's right. "No." To sex. That kind of sex, anyway. *Intercourse.*

KAREN Which rules out pretty much everything we can do but that's fine . . . "no" it is. (*To* BEV) Can he eat me out?

BEV . . . oh Jesus . . . I don't know!

KAREN "Yes" or "no?"

BEV Then "yes." That's alright, I suppose . . .

STEVE Sure, *that's* fine. Of course the *lezzie* stuff is gonna be okay . . .

BEV What's that?

STEVE Nothing.

BEV No, you know what . . . you've been making an unending series of sly little remarks all night, so why don't you just say what you wanna say to me, Steve? (*Beat.*) Go ahead.

STEVE . . . we should probably just leave it for now . . .

BEV No, why don't we get this . . . *thing* . . . out that's between us and then we can go on from there. (*Beat.*) Go on.

STEVE Listen, you don't wanna hear what I think about your . . . *lifestyle* . . . and I don't need to hear what you've got to say about . . .

BEV My "lifestyle?" You mean the fact that I am a lesbian? That I love women?

STEVE Yeah, that and . . . you know. Other stuff.

BEV How would *that* possibly have anything to do with you? Hmm?

STEVE It doesn't! You can eat all the pussy you want, like a hungry little beaver. I don't give a shit, Bev!

KAREN Can we not do this right now?

STEVE No, sorry, Karen, but this bitch has been *begging* for it since I walked in the door and now I'm . . . gonna . . .

BEV What? You're gonna what?!

STEVE Nothing! Fuck this! (*To* MISSY.) Let's go!

KAREN Great! (*To* BEV.) *Now* you've done it! Right when I actually *need* you, you go and . . .

BEV "I've" done it?! What about *this* guy?!

STEVE Fuck you!

BEV Fuck *you*! (*To* KAREN.) Why do you always have to take somebody else's side whenever we argue?! I don't get it!!

KAREN I don't do that!

BEV ALWAYS!

STEVE *stops short and turns back to* KAREN *and* BEV; MISSY *bumps into him and waits to hear what's next.*

STEVE I don't know how you do it! I mean it, I really don't . . . (*To* BEV.) If Missy said half the shit to me that you do to Karen, I'd be in *Vegas* divorcing her ass by, like, 9:30 tonight. The *latest*.

BEV Is that right?

STEVE Too fucking true! (*To* MISSY.) No *offense*, sweetie.

BEV Well, well, well . . .

STEVE And *that's* because you're a chick! If we were here and Karen was married—and I'm talking about actually married, not some bogus ceremony on a *cliff-side* somewhere so you can be included in her benefits—then I'd give you a real piece of my mind. (*To* KAREN.) You used to be, didn't ya, to that one . . . basketball guy? Married?

KAREN For about a year, yeah.

MISSY Just like us! (*Pumps her fist.*) WOO-HOO!

STEVE & KAREN Shhhhh.

STEVE Seriously, though, if it was him here and he was going on *half* as much as you have— and that dude was big, not freakish, like *Manute Bol* or anything, but a big dude—I would've climbed on a chair and punched him in the mouth by now, swear to God!

BEV Really?

STEVE Hell yeah! Straight in the kisser. You go and treat someone you love like shit . . . and *in* public? (*Gestures.*) BAM! Right in those ugly lips of yours . . .

BEV Don't let that stop you.

STEVE Huh? (*Turning to her.*) What'd you say?

BEV I said "don't let that stop you." If you wanna hit me, then go ahead. Don't let my being a woman stop you . . .

STEVE Sweetheart, I'm more of a woman than you will *ever* be, so . . .

BEV Talk is cheap, asshole.

STEVE Hey, you know what . . . ?

BEV Come on, fuckface!

STEVE Don't tempt me, rug muncher!

BEV *and* STEVE *get right up in each other's faces now—*KAREN *jumps in, doing her best to try and keep peace.*

KAREN Bev! Steve! (*To* MISSY.) Missy, would you help me, please!!

MISSY No, come on . . . let 'em get it out.

KAREN Oh yeah, great idea!

BEV You fucking bastard! You prick!!

STEVE Fuck you! Sticks and stones, bitch! Sticks and stones!!

BEV Shithead! Fucking no-talent . . . loser!

STEVE That's right!! I might not have much talent and I'm whatever . . . getting a bit older and my movies don't make the same dent in the box office as before, but you know what, *Bev*? I can walk out that door right there—a door that somebody else paid for—and before I get to my *Ferrari* someone will recognize me or honk their horn or ask for my autograph. I am *some*body to *every*body!!! People know me . . . but who the fuck are you? Hmm? *Who*? They can't even get your name right on a piece-a-shit indie about high school chicks licking each other out! *That's* who you are. A nobody.

That's it: BEV *pushes* STEVE *and he reacts. Goes for her.*

BEV Take your best shot!

STEVE I would never hit a woman—not even one like you!

BEV That's because you're afraid of me!

STEVE It's because I don't wanna *touch* you!!

KAREN Guys, stop this! STOP!

BEV You wanna wrestle, how about that?!

STEVE What?!

BEV If you're so afraid to punch me then let's wrestle . . . *if* you're man enough! *If* you've got the *balls*!!

STEVE Don't tempt me, you shrub scout . . .!

BEV Come on! (*Kicks* STEVE *in the shin.*) Do it!

STEVE OWWW! You stupid . . . fucking . . .!

BEV I'll kick your ass!

STEVE You're crazy! (*To* KAREN.) Your girlfriend is fucking nuts, Karen!!

BEV Pussy!

STEVE Shut up! (*To* KAREN.) Tell her to shut up or I'm gonnna . . . I *swear* I'm gonna . . . !

BEV What?! You're gonna *what*?!

KAREN Steve, I'm begging you to . . . please stop! Bev, stop it now! STOP!!

BEV No! This guy struts around here, acting like he actually *means* something because he can stand in front of an audience without pissing himself and I, for one, am sick of it!

STEVE *You* try doing it, you little muff-diver!

BEV I did! In *second* grade!

STEVE I really should smash you one, I swear to God! You little bush-licker!!

BEV Do it! *Do* it!! I *dare* you!!

KAREN You guys, stop it! Stop!! I'm asking you nicely now, so please . . . stop this . . .

BEV Let's quit playing and just do this! Come on! (*Gestures.*) Let's *wrestle*, you and me!

STEVE Hey, hey . . . this isn't some high school crap where the coach *has* to allow you on the team . . . I'd kick your ass, you fucking lesbo!

BEV *Prove* it, limp dick!

STEVE I should, I really should!

KAREN . . . guys, *please* . . . you're driving me crazy!

STEVE I oughta give you a real taste of some . . . cock in your mouth . . .

BEV Yeah? You and whose cock?

STEVE Fuck you!

BEV Fuck you!!

STEVE Fine! Let's do it!

BEV Fine!

STEVE Missy! (*Gesturing.*) Hold my necklace . . .

KAREN Jesus.

MISSY Sure, sweetie. (*To the others.*) That's a real shark's tooth. I got it for him in *Australia* . . .

STEVE *and* BEV *start backing slowly away from each other.*

KAREN Seriously . . . what's going on *now*?

BEV I'm gonna kick this motherfucker's ass that's what's going on now. Make some room!

STEVE I'm gonna knock that smile off your dyke-y girlfriend's nasty little mouth because she won't shut her goddamn trap! (*To* KAREN.) No offense . . .

KAREN . . . I give up.

BEV Then sit and watch, Karen. Sit and watch. (*To* STEVE.) I'm gonna enjoy this . . .

STEVE Live and learn, that's what you should be saying because that's what you're about to do, you little fish-eater: "Live and learn."

BEV *moves furniture aside to make space.* STEVE *helps out.*

KAREN . . . I can't believe this . . .

BEV Asshole's not gonna believe it, either, in about *two* minutes . . .

STEVE Wow, you are just *begging* for a beating and I'm gonna give it to you, sister . . .

BEV Bring it, fuck bucket.

STEVE Happy to, super twat . . . we gonna wager anything on it or is it just a gentlemen's bet?

They have a usable spot now and the two combatants start to circle each other again. Hissing and spitting.

BEV Whatever you want.

STEVE Hmmmm . . . if we're gonna do it, we might as well make it interesting.

BEV This is gonna be sweet! (*To* STEVE.) Anything you like . . .

STEVE Yeah?

BEV *Any*thing. Go for it.

STEVE No, no . . . ladies first. I insist. (*Beat.*) Oh wait, I don't see any *ladies* here . . . just you! (*Laughs.*) *Snatch*!

BEV Fine . . . you win, the two of you can do whatever you want on camera. Fuck yourselves silly and I won't say a word . . .

STEVE Good, because I hate the sound of your fucking *voice*! (*Beat.*) And? AND?!

BEV *And* if I win . . . then we march upstairs and we do the very same thing . . . right here. Right now.

KAREN . . . Bev . . .

BEV Stay outta this, Karen! (*To* STEVE.) Now, do we have a bet . . .?

STEVE . . . what?

BEV You heard me!

STEVE Why would I ever want to . . .? (*Beat.*) Ohh, wait, no, now I see! Now I see! You *lured* me here so I could . . . you want me to father your kid . . . right? Right?! (*Beat.*) No way!! That is so . . . fucking . . . creepy!!!

BEV I wasn't looking at you, Steve.

She turns slightly toward MISSY. *The others turn as well.* MISSY's *eyes go wide as she suddenly understands the bet.*

STEVE Wait . . . *what*?!

KAREN You mean . . .?

BEV Yes. I mean Missy and myself . . . (*Beat.*) After all, fair's fair.

STEVE Are you crazy?! I mean, that's . . . *no* way! (*Beat.*) That's my *wife*!!

KAREN You guys, stop! This is insane!

BEV I'm only gonna do it if this blow-hard is brave enough to take me on . . . personally, I think he's gonna wuss out on us here . . . (*To* KAREN.) . . . and it's no more insane than what you're proposing. Less, really. At least *I'm* attracted to her . . . at least I'll enjoy it, instead of doing it just to be more famous! *That's* insane!!

STEVE Fuck-you, Gertrude Stein . . .

BEV Ohhh, good one! That's a big name for someone who doesn't even know where *Belgium* is!

STEVE Eat shit! (*Pulls his shirt off.*) I had to read some of her poems in school . . . or a *quote* or something . . . and I never forget a face. Especially a big, fat . . . ugly one like hers!

BEV You know what? (*Pulls off her shirt.*) You really deserve this . . . and I'm gonna enjoy giving it to ya, but first things first: do you agree? (*Points.*) DO YOU?! Come on, big man, yes or no?! *Yes* or *no*?!!

STEVE God! You fucking . . . yes! *YES, YES, YES*!!

MISSY Wait, no . . .

STEVE Come on! Let's just do this!! If I lose you can have Missy!!

MISSY No, I don't think that's very . . .

STEVE Don't worry, babe . . . you're totally safe! No way she can beat me! Show me what you got, bull-dyke . . .

BEV *moves into a crouch.* STEVE *does exactly the same.*

BEV Here I come, spray tan . . . watch out!

STEVE *makes a clumsy lunge and* BEV *goes under it, using his own weight to pick him up and throw him down. Wham!*

BEV You enjoy that?!

STEVE Fuck off, you freak! Come on!! (*She lunges.*) Whoa! Whoa! Wait now . . . how do we get a clear winner here?

BEV What?

STEVE I don't want you cheating your way outta this thing . . . how is the winner declared?

BEV By one person getting pinned or tapping out! Duh!! How *else* would we do it?!

STEVE I'm fine with that! Just wanted to be sure!

BEV Quit stalling, you big, stupid . . . and you're on bottoms, by the way, so get down there . . .

STEVE What?!

BEV I had first blood . . . knocked you to the ground, so now we start on the floor. You're down on the mat.

STEVE No, it's . . . fuck that! You can . . . it's just gotta be a *neutral* starting position! We can circle each other . . . and then . . .

BEV If you really knew how to wrestle, you'd know it's true . . . come on, get going!

STEVE Uh-uh . . . no fair! No fair!

KAREN Bev should know . . . she wrestled at state.

STEVE *What*?! What're you, kidding . . .?

BEV Nope. Spring of '93.

KAREN It was on the cover of *Sports Illlustrated* and everything . . .

STEVE So what? What does that prove?

BEV It proves I know the rules of wrestling, so get your skinny ass on the floor so I can finish you off!

STEVE Hold on! I wanna look this up! (*Pulls out his iPhone.*) My battery's dead. Shit! (*To* MISSY.) Missy, gimme your phone.

MISSY *suddenly springs into action, racing* STEVE *to her purse. She gets there a second faster.*

MISSY I'll do it!

STEVE What're you . . . just let me . . .

MISSY No, I've got it, babe, *hold* on!

She pulls her bag away from him but STEVE *holds on. The contents dump out onto the patio. Shrimp puffs and all.*

STEVE What-the-fuck? (*Looks at her.*) *Missy?*

MISSY Sweetie . . . I was hungry.

STEVE You know what? I'm surrounded! I am just fucking *surrounded*! (*To all of them.*) *This* is the reason we secretly hate you guys—and I mean all of you now, *all* women, not just the lesbians and ugly chicks but all of you! (*Beat.*) I mean, shit, you are the most deceptive bunch of . . . *whores* . . . it's unbeliev-able! *This* is why we cheat on you and wanna fuck you in the ass so much . . . all of man's bad behavior is payback for this kind of bullshit right here! You're a pack of, of, of . . . *vipers,* that's what you are. Impossible to trust, from our mothers right down to our death beds!! (*To* MISSY.) You think I do this shit . . . buy ya stuff and introduce you to people and all that . . . help keep you looking good just for *me*? Huh? It's for you!! For *you.* And this is how you're gonna repay me?!! Lying and . . . and . . . sneaking food . . . God, I feel like that one dude . . . from Greek history—that king I almost played in *Troy* except they went with that one big Irish fucker, whatever his name is . . . I feel just like him now!

STEVE *throws* MISSY's *bag down in disgust and kicks it aside.* MISSY *tries to plead her case:*

MISSY . . . I just wanted another shrimp puff . . .

STEVE Yeah, well, don't come crying to me when they got a picture of your saggy ass on the cover of *The Enquirer,* okay, 'cause I'll be laughing in your face! (*Stomps his feet.*) You hear me . . . *in* your face!!

KAREN I don't understand . . . what does a Greek king have to do with anything?

STEVE Jesus, Karen, you're *so* . . . I mean, I like working with you and everything, but you are a little bit ignorant!

KAREN Hey, *don't* snap at me! I just asked you a question . . .

STEVE Maybe if you'd stop *branding* yourself for five minutes you'd know what the hell I'm talking about!

KAREN I'm not *branding* myself . . . I am *trying* to leave an entertainment and retail *legacy* behind me, thank you very much, Steve!!

BEV I got a Masters in classical literature, Steve, and I don't know what you're referring to, either . . . and Brian Cox is *Scottish*, not Irish. "Look it up!"

STEVE Whatever! I don't care what country he's from! It doesn't matter!! I brought it up as a . . . because I'm . . . I'm making a . . . Fuck!! It's a *comparison*!! *You* look it up if you're just so goddamn interested!!

He quickly digs in MISSY*'s purse and pulls out a pretty pink phone with rhinestones on it. He tosses it to* BEV.

BEV No. (*Puts the phone aside.*) After.

STEVE "After" what?

BEV *After* I kick your ass.

STEVE Lady . . . I'm gonna enjoy this, and I don't even give a damn if you've got the rules right or not. (*Beat.*) Come on!

STEVE *gets down on the ground on all fours.* BEV *drops to one knee next to him.*

BEV Somebody call it!

KAREN What?

BEV Someone say "go!"

KAREN . . . but . . .

BEV Do it! Do-it-now!

STEVE I got it! His name was "Agamemnon!"

MISSY GO!

BEV *explodes like a champion, grabbing* STEVE *by a wrist and flipping him on his back. Drives him to the floor.* BEV *spins* STEVE *around but he breaks a hold and gets to his feet.*

STEVE Take that! Point for me!

BEV We're not doing points!

KAREN Bev says no points.

STEVE Fine, then, it's an *escape* and we have to start down again!
    And you've got bottoms this time!

BEV Fine! Whatever!

Into the crouch they go again, this time with the roles reversed. STEVE *is poised while* BEV's *as tight as a wire.*

STEVE Come on, fuck! Call it! Makes me sick being this close to
    her . . .

BEV . . . my God, you're a shitbag!

KAREN Should we say go?

MISSY GO!

STEVE *moves quickly but not fast enough*—BEV *does a low roll and is suddenly on top of and behind* STEVE.

BEV How do you like *that*? Huh?

STEVE What the fuck!

BEV OOOOOHH! What a good boy! You're *such* a good boy!

KAREN Wow! Good one, honey!

BEV . . . thanks . . .

STEVE Shut up! I thought you were against this, Karen!

BEV *and* STEVE *grapple throughout the following exchange:*

KAREN I am, but that was cool . . .

STEVE Escape!

KAREN Keep the pressure on!

STEVE Shhh! I can't concentrate! (*To* BEV.) Stop moving so much, you squirrely . . . little . . .

BEV You're getting tired, old man . . .

STEVE I'm not *old*! I'm . . . 48 . . .

BEV Bullshit.

STEVE I am! Shut up, shut up, shut the fuck up!

BEV Oww! You can't do that!!

KAREN *and* MISSY *edge closer—trying to watch but be safe.*

KAREN Be careful!

STEVE It's not my fault she has tits!

KAREN . . . just don't hurt each other . . .

STEVE Bit late for that now! (*Beat.*) Awwwh!

BEV Totally legal move!

STEVE You did that on purpose . . . hit my crotch!

BEV It's not my fault you've got a cock!

STEVE *You* wish you had a cock! (*To* MISSY.) Feel free to shout out a touch of *encouragement*, sweetie! Shit!!

MISSY Sorry . . . (*Without much effort.*) Go, Steve.

STEVE Great, thanks! (*To* BEV.) Stop with . . . all the . . . ouch! You're *choking* me!!

BEV You like that position?! You want to put it on the list?! Huh?!

STEVE I can't breathe . . . you . . . fucking . . . pig . . .

STEVE *manages to break free, coughing and clutching at his throat.*

BEV *springs onto* STEVE's *back and brings him down again. She turns him over and has him in a cradle in three swift moves. He is pinned.*

BEV Somebody call it! Hurry up!

KAREN What? I don't know how . . . to . . .

BEV Get on your knees and see if you can see that his shoulders . . .

KAREN Sweetie, this is a new dress.

BEV ARE HIS SHOULDERS ON THE GROUND?! HURRY!!

KAREN *gets down on the ground, trying not to ruin her new outfit. She looks at the pair of them.*

STEVE . . . lemme go . . . you . . . lezzie . . .

BEV Honey, call it! Come on!!

STEVE Ok, ok . . . stop now . . . Uncle . . . *Uncle*!!

BEV Not until she calls it . . . (*To* KAREN.) Karen, call it!

KAREN But his one shoulder's . . . I can see . . .

MISSY *jumps down on the ground and pushes* KAREN *out of the way. She takes a quick look, then slaps her hand on the patio tile. Bam!*

MISSY Pinned!

BEV *instantly breaks free and jumps to her feet. She grabs* MISSY's *phone and tosses it onto* STEVE's *chest.*

BEV "Suck on *that*, you little bitch!" You just got beat by a girl . . .

STEVE That's . . . I wasn't ready for . . . (*To* KAREN.) She's not even a

woman! Nobody can just do that without . . . (*To* BEV.) You might
as well be a *dude*! I mean, what the fuck . . .?

STEVE *pulls himself to his feet, grumbling and coughing.*

BEV Yeah, I might as well be . . . but I'm *not*! I'm Beverly Williams
and I just kicked your ass, Steve. So there. (*Points.*) Now sit
yourself down and wait for me and that beautiful wife of yours to
come back downstairs . . .

KAREN Bev?

BEV You hear me?

STEVE . . .

BEV I said: did-you-hear-me? (*Yells.*) STEVE!

STEVE But I'm . . . I didn't even get a chance to— (*To* MISSY.) Missy?
Baby? You're not *really* gonna do this, right? I mean . . .

MISSY You lost, sweetie. (*Beat.*) I gotta go.

STEVE . . . but this is . . . *no* . . . this is . . .

BEV . . . you guys wanna make up a quick list of what we can and
can't do up there? Hmmm? "Sixty-nine?" No? "A strap-on?"
Nothing?

STEVE No, wait . . . that's . . . this is fucked!

KAREN Bev, I beg you . . . do not do this!! Please-don't-do-this to
me!!

STEVE . . . no! This is not gonna happen! (*Beat.*) Missy, I forbid
you! You hear me?!! You are forbidden to step inside that house!
Seriously . . .

MISSY You should've thought about that before you offered me up.
As a *prize*.

STEVE Honey . . . what does that even mean?

MISSY You know what it means, baby. You do anything you want,
always, and if I wanna go with you or tag along, well, that's fine—

you *allow* me to be your *plus one*. (*Beat.*) But this time it's gonna cost you . . .

STEVE That's not true . . . hey, I love you.

MISSY I know you do, but that doesn't make it not true. I'm always an afterthought . . . you call me your "wife," but . . . I dunno.

STEVE Missy! No! Wait! Baby . . . this isn't right. I'm not gonna let you . . . just . . . I forbid this. (*Beat.*) Did you hear me? I said "I *forbid* this." Now get in the car . . .

MISSY Steve . . . stop! You need to understand what you've done here: you *used* me . . . the woman you *married* . . . and this is the consequence of that. *This* is what you did. (*Beat.*) And we don't have a pre-nup, either, just in case you've forgotten, so don't be thinking too hard about driving to Vegas to *divorce* my ass, 'cause *that'll* cost you, too. A shitload. Actually, it's kinda funny . . .

MISSY *drops* STEVE*'s necklace in his lap, then turns and looks at the others. She takes a deep breath. Smiles.*

STEVE What is?

MISSY . . . tonight you're *my* "plus one." (*To* BEV.) We should go now. I'm hungry.

BEV *smiles broadly for once—she too has a pretty smile—she turns and watches* MISSY *disappear inside the house.* BEV *is about to go in herself when* KAREN *moves to her.*

KAREN Sweetheart, I'm sorry. I didn't . . . I mean, I never meant for this to . . .

BEV What? *Hurt* me? (*Beat.*) People rarely mean to hurt each other, but they still do . . . they do it and they keep right on going.

KAREN I know. I know that *now.*

BEV And the next time I pull you aside and say shit like "hey, I know it sucks but we need to discuss stuff more?" *This*, right here, is the kind of thing that I'm talking about . . . (*To* STEVE.) Oh, and Steve: cause and effect? It's spelled with an "e." Effect. C & E. Just so you know.

BEV *smiles at* STEVE. *She turns and touches* KAREN*'s face with her hand, then walks off. Into the house.*

STEVE I'm gonna look that up . . .

KAREN What just happened? What just happened here? (*Beat.*) Steve?

STEVE *doesn't find this funny. Not even just a tiny bit.*

STEVE I don't know. (*Beat.*) *Fuck.*

STEVE *stands, checks his phone. Battery is still dead.*

KAREN This is *not* how I saw the evening going! Maybe I should go in, check on dinner.

STEVE That's ok. I'm not hungry now. (*Beat.*) Should we . . . maybe . . .?

KAREN What?

STEVE I dunno! Go spy on 'em or . . . that sorta thing? See what they're up to?

KAREN No thanks.

STEVE You're not curious?

KAREN No way! I don't wanna know what they do up there. Or how many times *or* what with.

From an open window above them, a soft moaning begins. It builds throughout.

KAREN . . . oh for God's sake!

STEVE *Really?* Is that necessary? Jesus . . . we're right here.

KAREN *Now* what?

STEVE I dunno. I mean . . .

STEVE *nods at this and sits back a bit. Defeated. He puts his necklace back on. Checks his watch.*

STEVE . . . shit! Tonight sucks! (*Beat.*) *And* I forgot to *tweet* earlier . . . when I was at the Apple Store! Fuck! How could I forget to do that?!!

On instinct he pulls his iPhone out, checks it. Battery is still dead. He spots MISSY's *phone and crosses to it.*

KAREN God, I *never* forget to tweet! Not ever. It makes me feel *connected.*

He picks up MISSY's *phone while listening to* KAREN. *Sets it back down.*

STEVE Screw it . . . I'll pretend I'm there later. The Apple Store's open late. (*Beat.*) So I guess we should just . . . what? God, what do people *do* in situations like this?!

KAREN I'm not sure.

STEVE Yeah, me neither . . .

A pause as they look at each other, completely unsure of how the "little people" spend their time.

KAREN I suppose we . . . could . . . ummmm . . .

STEVE What?

KAREN I dunno. (*Beat.*) We could always . . . just . . . talk.

STEVE "Talk?"

KAREN Yes. I say something, then you, and then me again . . . and, you know . . . we "talk."

STEVE What . . . you mean, like . . . to *each other*?

KAREN I guess so.

STEVE Oh.

KAREN We don't have to. I was . . . only . . .

STEVE No, it's . . . fine. No. We can talk. (*Beat.*) Sure, why not?

KAREN Ok.

STEVE Yeah. (*Beat.*) . . . let's talk.

Silence now as KAREN *struggles to come up with a subject.* STEVE *keeps glancing up at the open window.*

They sit there, searching for something to say. A word. A sentence. Anything.

More groans from above. Faster now, gaining in intensity. Blasts of light go off, like a sea of flashbulbs. The two actors are frozen in the glare for a moment. Lights fade as they remain in this pose for a second longer, like a Polaroid developing.

Sounds from the night growing in the background. Animals and traffic and dark things. It is a wild and beautiful sound. Drowning out everything else.

Silence. Darkness.

ALSO BY NEIL LABUTE AND AVAILABLE FROM THE OVERLOOK PRESS

"THE MOST LEGITIMATELY PROVOCATIVE AND POLARIZING PLAYWRIGHT AT WORK TODAY." —DAVID AMSDEN, *NEW YORK*

REASONS TO BE HAPPY

A PLAY BY NEIL LaBUTE

In the companion piece to Neil LaBute's 2009 Tony-nominated *Reasons to be Pretty*, Greg, Steph, Carly, and Kent pick up their lives three years later, but in different romantic pairings, as they each search desperately for that elusive object of desire: happiness.

"Mr. LaBute is more relaxed as a playwright than he's ever been. He is clearly having a good time revisiting old friends . . . you're likely to feel the same way . . . the most winning romantic comedy of the summer, replete with love talk, LaBute-style, which isn't so far from hate talk . . . " —**Ben Brantley, *The New York Times***

$14.95 978-1-4683-0721-4